Casual Entertaining

GENERAL EDITOR
CHUCK WILLIAMS

RECIPES
JOYCE GOLDSTEIN AND OTHER CONTRIBUTORS

PHOTOGRAPHY
ALLAN ROSENBERG AND ALLEN V. LOTT

TIME
LIFE
BOOKS

TIME-LIFE BOOKS

Time-Life Books is a division of Time Life Inc.

Time-Life is a trademark of Time-Warner Inc. U.S.A.

Time-Life Custom Publishing
Vice President and Publisher: Terry Newell
Managing Editor: Donia Ann Steele
Director of Acquisitions: Jennifer L. Pearce
Vice President of Sales and Marketing: Neil Levin
Director of Financial Operations: J. Brian Birky

WILLIAMS-SONOMA
Founder and Vice Chairman: Chuck Williams
Book Buyer: Victoria Kalish

WELDON OWEN INC.
President: John Owen
Vice President and Publisher: Wendely Harvey
Chief Operating Officer: Larry Partington
Vice President International Sales: Stuart Laurence
Managing Editor: Judith Dunham
Consulting Editor: Norman Kolpas
Copy Editor: Sharon Silva
Design: John Bull, The Book Design Company
Production Director: Stephanie Sherman
Production Consultant: Sarah Lemas
Production Manager: Jen Dalton
Production Editor: Deborah Cowder
Food Photographer: Allan Rosenberg
Additional Photography: Allen V. Lott
Food Stylists: Heidi Gintner, Susan Massey,
    John Phillip Carroll, Peggy Fallon
Prop Stylist: Sandra Griswold
Illustrations: Alice Harth

The Williams-Sonoma Kitchen Library
conceived and produced by Weldon Owen Inc.
814 Montgomery St., San Francisco, CA 94133

In collaboration with Williams-Sonoma
3250 Van Ness Ave., San Francisco, CA 94109

Printed in China by Toppan Printing Co., LTD.

A Note on Weights and Measures:
All recipes include customary U.S. and metric
measurements. Metric conversions are based on
a standard developed for these books and have
been rounded off. Actual weights may vary.

A Weldon Owen Production

Copyright © 1998 Weldon Owen Inc.
Reprinted in 1998
All rights reserved, including the right of
reproduction in whole or in part in any form.

Library of Congress
Cataloging-in-Publication Data:

Goldstein, Joyce Esersky.
    Casual entertaining / [recipes, Joyce Goldstein] ; general editor,
Chuck Williams ; photography, Allan Rosenberg and Allen V. Lott.
        p.   cm. — (Williams-Sonoma kitchen library)
    Includes index.
    ISBN 0-7370-2000-8
    1. Entertaining.   2. Cookery.   I. Williams, Chuck.   II. Title.
III. Series.
TX731.G565   1998
641.5—dc21   96-9543
                                                                 CIP

Contents

STARTERS 15

SALADS & SIDE DISHES 33

MAIN COURSES 57

DESSERTS 83

INTRODUCTION

I am always surprised when I hear people say that the thought of entertaining makes them feel intimidated. For me, preparing a meal for friends is one of life's greatest pleasures.

Maybe I feel this way because I have always taken what you might call a casual approach to parties. "Casual" doesn't imply that I don't plan the event, serve good food, or set an attractive table. Rather, by "casual," I mean that I like to entertain in a relaxed style, with a sense of ease that extends from the menu, through the table settings and decorations, to the mood of the gathering itself.

Any gathering, regardless of the season, event, or size of guest list, can be casual. Wherever you live and whatever your means, this book will help you put together a meal with an air of informality that lets everyone involved— including you, the person who cooks the meal—relax, from the moment the occasion is planned until the last person leaves and the final dish has been stacked in the cupboard.

Whether you're giving a party to mark a birthday or an anniversary or just inviting a few people over for Sunday supper, the introductory pages that follow are geared toward making your casual entertaining easier and more enjoyable. They are followed by 45 recipes that will help you plan an event that is truly stylish and memorable.

Chuck Williams

CASUAL ENTERTAINING BASICS

The words *casual entertaining* can take on many different meanings, from a backyard barbecue to a weeknight supper to a birthday party. What all such occasions have in common is easy hospitality and the pleasure that comes whenever good food is generously shared.

Even though casual meals may be far more relaxed than formal parties, they still call for thought and planning, beginning with the menu itself (opposite). Next comes deciding where to hold the party and how to set and decorate the table.

Let your imagination—and your home—dictate where you will present the meal. Your dining room is the obvious choice. But some gatherings feel warmer and more spontaneous when held in a spacious kitchen or cozy family room. Sunny weather might invite a move to a patio or balcony, while a chilly day might steer you toward a fireplace. The mood you are aiming for, as well as the recipes and the size of the party, will determine whether you serve the food on individual plates arranged in the kitchen, from bowls and platters at the dining table, or buffet style.

Throughout this book, a variety of dishware, glassware, and cutlery is used in the photographs, each kind chosen to match the food and create a sense of occasion. Let these selections inspire your own table-setting choices. Work first with what you have, then combine different patterns, or borrow or buy additional pieces. That same spirit of flexibility, ease, and appropriateness also applies to your choice of decorations, particularly flowers. (For a guide to setting the table and arranging flowers, see pages 8–12.) Don't forget the contribution that candles and music can also make to the mood.

PLANNING MENUS

Once you have invited your guests, browse through the recipes in this book to begin planning your menu, keeping in mind the type of party you desire and your guests' personal tastes. Then choose starters, main courses, side dishes, and desserts to suit the occasion. (Bear in mind that you may have to adjust ingredient quantities of individual recipes to yield the number of servings required.) The four menus given below only begin to suggest the myriad possibilities.

❖ *WEEKDAY SUPPER FOR FRIENDS* ❖

Lentil Soup

White Fish with Moroccan Spice Marinade

Moroccan Vegetables

Dried Apricot Compote

❖ *SUNDAY FAMILY-STYLE DINNER* ❖

Tomato Salad with Basil-Honey Vinaigrette

Roasted Rosemary Chicken

Potato and Onion Gratin

Bing Cherry Cheese Tart

❖ *HOMECOMING CELEBRATION* ❖

Deviled Crab Cakes with Ginger-Citrus Vinaigrette

Roast Leg of Lamb with Braised Garlic, Sherry, and Thyme

Glazed Carrots with Grapes and Walnuts

Chocolate Mousse

❖ *CASUAL MEDITERRANEAN FEAST* ❖

Roasted Eggplant with Pita

Greek Beef Stew

Rice Pilaf with Dried Apricots, Slivered Almonds, and Mint

Hazelnut Biscotti

SETTING THE TABLE

No matter how casual the occasion, every conscientious host or hostess wants to make a good impression. The simplest way to do so is with your table setting. From your everyday tableware, select cutlery, dishes, glasses, and napkins that not only complement one another but also are compatible with the food being served.

For most occasions, you will want to fold the napkins into neat triangles or rectangles, placing them to the left of the serving plate—beneath or just to the left of the forks. Remember to orient the napkin with its folded edge facing the plate, making it all the easier for a guest to pick the napkin up by a corner, open it, and drape it over the lap. (For a more stylish decorative effect, try the napkin-folding techniques demonstrated on pages 9–10.)

If you want to avoid unnecessary clutter, bring any other items to the table only as needed. Dessert forks or spoons, for example, would be placed on the table along with dessert plates after the main course has been cleared.

FOLDING NAPKINS

The basic, casual-style techniques illustrated on these pages show how, with just a few simple steps, table linens can be easily transformed into attractive decorations. Both are based on standard, 20-inch (50-cm) square napkins.

Some decorative techniques take a little more time than folding a napkin into the triangle shown in the setting opposite. For example, using that same triangle, roll it up from the tip of the right angle to the long folded edge and then tie a loose knot in the center. You now have a jaunty, informal bowtie to place atop a plate. It takes only a few extra moments to achieve even more dazzling, but no less casual, effects like the bouquet and pointed pocket folds demonstrated here and on page 10.

CREATING A BOUQUET

A bouquetlike arrangement can be made by folding together two napkins of complementary or contrasting colors and patterns and securing them with a napkin ring. The completed bouquet is placed to the left of or on the dinner plate.

1. Open both napkins. Place one napkin on a flat surface and set the other on top at a 45-degree angle to form an eight-pointed star.

2. Using your fingertips, grasp the centers of the two napkins and pick them up.

3. Arrange the points and sides of the two napkins into neat overlapping folds. Insert the stem of the bouquet into a napkin ring and pull almost halfway through. Adjust the points into a full, attractive bouquet.

MAKING A POINTED POCKET

Folded and tied into a compact pocket, a napkin also serves as a creative holder for a set of flatware. It makes an especially convenient bundle for guests to pick up at a buffet table.

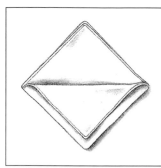

2. Fold the point of the topmost layer downward until it almost—but not quite—touches the bottom corner.

1. Open the napkin flat, then fold it into quarters. Rotate it so the open points are at the top.

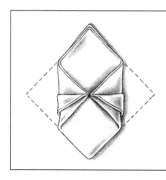

3. Turn the napkin over, keeping the open points at the top. Fold the two side corners inward so they meet in the center.

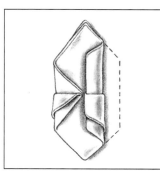

4. Carefully holding the napkin in place, fold the sides inward again so they meet in the center.

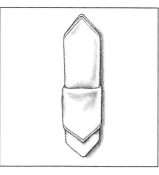

5. Holding the folds in place, turn the napkin over to reveal the pocket. Tie a piece of raffia or ribbon around the napkin just below the pocket. Tuck the cutlery into the pocket.

ARRANGING FLOWERS

For most casual occasions, you will want to use a small bouquet or two of seasonal flowers simply arranged in vases or other suitable containers, like the gerbera daisies on page 6. The size of each bouquet, the vase you choose, and where you place the arrangement on the table should show the flowers off at their best without distracting guests' attention or blocking their view of one another across the table.

For certain occasions, you may want to create a more unusual centerpiece or decoration for a buffet table, side table, entranceway, or mantel. These centerpieces should also use flowers or plants at their seasonal peak. The arrangements shown here add a special touch while maintaining an appropriately informal tone.

SWAGGING A FLOWERPOT

Small potted plants you already have growing in your home—or plants purchased from a nursery or florist—easily become appealing living decorations when rimmed with fabric. The fabric serves to hide the soil as well as to frame the plant attractively.

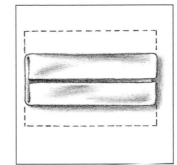

1. Cut fabric as long as twice the circumference of the rim of the pot and 12 inches (30 cm) wide. Place the fabric wrong side up, fold both sides into the center, and secure the seam with masking tape.

2. Using a ruler and pencil, mark the masking tape in the middle and 2 inches (5 cm) from each end. Mark the remaining length of tape at regular intervals of 2–3 inches (5–7.5 cm).

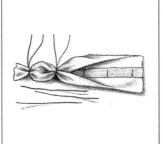

3. Cut a 6-inch (15-cm) length of florist's wire for every mark on the tape. Gather the fabric together at each mark, concealing the masking tape, and lightly twist a piece of wire around the gather to secure it in place.

4. Starting at one end of the swag, secure the ends of a wire twist inside the rim of the pot with masking tape. Continue tucking the swag around the pot and securing the wires inside. Place the plant inside the swagged pot.

COMBINING FLOWERS, FRUIT, AND FOLIAGE

Arranged in a container scaled to the setting, flowers, small fruit, and foliage may be grouped to form a natural-looking centerpiece. Here, garden roses, tulips, and freesias are combined with kumquats wired onto several pear branches.

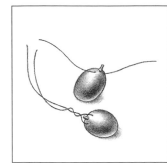

1. Cut a 6-inch (15-cm) length of florist's wire for each piece of fruit. Pierce the fruit near the stem end with the wire. Twist the wire together, making a knot close to the stem.

2. Attach each piece of fruit to a branch close to a cluster of leaves or to a small notch in the branch. Twist the wire around the branch to secure the fruit and hide the wire. Tie on as many pieces of fruit as you wish.

3. Cut florist's foam to fit snugly inside your chosen container. Immerse the foam in water for 5 minutes, then place in the container. Use a knife to peel off the bark from the bottom 2–3 inches (5–7.5 cm) of each branch. Insert the branches into the foam.

4. Fill in the gaps between branches with small groups of seasonal cut flowers. Add enough branches, arranging them as necessary, to form a well-balanced composition.

Chicken Stock

Homemade stock is always more flavorful than the powdered or canned alternatives. This stock can be made in advance stored in a covered container in the refrigerator for up to 4 days or in the freezer for up to 3 months.

2 lb (1 kg) chicken parts
3 fresh flat-leaf (Italian) parsley sprigs
2 fresh thyme sprigs
1 bay leaf
1 large yellow onion, coarsely chopped
1 or 2 carrots, peeled and chopped
1 celery stalk, chopped

Place the chicken parts in a large stockpot. Cover generously with water. Bring to a boil, regularly skimming off any foam and scum that forms on the surface. Cover, reduce the heat to medium-low, and simmer for about 1 hour.

Make a bouquet garni by combining the parsley and thyme sprigs and bay leaf on a small piece of cheesecloth (muslin) and bringing the corners together. Tie securely with kitchen string to form a small bag.

When the chicken has simmered for 1 hour, add the bouquet garni, onion, carrots, and celery, cover partially, and continue to simmer for 1½ hours longer.

Remove the stock from the heat and strain through a fine-mesh sieve or colander lined with a double thickness of cheesecloth and placed over a bowl. Remove the sieve or colander and discard the solids. Place the stock in the refrigerator. When the stock has cooled completely, skim off all the fat that has solidified on the top and store as directed above.

Makes 2–2½ qt (2–2.5 l)

Crostini

Use the crostini for garnishing soups or salads or to accompany Blue Cheese Spread with Walnuts (page 25). The crostini can also be sprinkled with chopped fresh herbs or rubbed with a garlic clove. You can top plain or seasoned crostini with purchased spreads such as olive (shown here), artichoke, or sundried tomato.

½ crusty French baguette or Italian coarse country
    bread, 2 inches (5 cm) in diameter and 10–12 inches
    (25–30 cm) long
extra-virgin olive oil

Positon a rack in the upper third of an oven and preheat to 450°F (230°C).

Using a sharp knife or a serrated bread knife, cut the bread on the diagonal into slices ½ inch (12 mm) thick. Brush each side lightly with olive oil and place on a baking sheet. Bake, turning once, until lightly golden, about 2 minutes on each side. Watch carefully and do not allow the crostini to toast until they are hard.

Remove from the oven and serve hot or at room temperature.

Makes 20–24 slices

Onion Tartlets

FOR THE DOUGH:

½ teaspoon sugar

¾ cup (6 fl oz/180 ml) warm water

1 package (2½ teaspoons) active
   dry yeast

2 cups (10 oz/315 g) all-purpose (plain)
   flour

1 teaspoon fine sea salt

2 tablespoons extra-virgin olive oil

½ cup (4 fl oz/125 ml) water

½ teaspoon sugar

salt and ground pepper to taste

1 lb (500 g) large yellow onions, thinly
   sliced and slivered

12 plump black olives, pitted and
   slivered

12 anchovy fillets in olive oil, drained
   and cut in half crosswise

½ cup (2 oz/60 g) pine nuts

*T*o make the dough, in a small bowl, stir the sugar into ½ cup (4 fl oz/120 ml) of the warm water. Sprinkle the yeast over the surface and let stand until bubbles start to rise, about 5 minutes. In a large bowl, stir together the flour and salt. Make a well in the center and add the yeast mixture to it along with the remaining ¼ cup (2 fl oz/60 ml) warm water. Using a wooden spoon, stir the liquid into the flour until all of the flour has been absorbed and a dough forms. Turn out onto a well-floured work surface and knead until smooth and elastic, 5–6 minutes. If the dough is sticky, add a little flour; if it is too dry, add a few drops of water. Shape into a ball, place in a floured bowl, and cover the bowl with a kitchen towel. Let stand in a warm place until doubled in bulk, about 12 hours.

Punch down the dough and turn out onto a lightly floured work surface. Knead for about 3 minutes, then roll out ⅓ inch (1 cm) thick. Using a round pastry cutter 1½ inches (4 cm) in diameter, cut out 24 rounds. Roll out these rounds again until they are about ⅛ inch (3 mm) thick. Lay the rounds on a nonstick baking sheet. (Store any leftover dough in a tightly sealed plastic bag in the refrigerator for another use.)

Combine the oil and water in a nonstick frying pan. Add the sugar, salt, and pepper. Bring to a boil and add the onions. Cover and cook over gentle heat, stirring from time to time, until the onions are golden and the water evaporates, about 20 minutes. Remove from the heat. Add the olives, anchovies, and pine nuts to the onions and mix well. Divide the onion mixture evenly among the dough rounds.

Bake until the topping and the edges of the pastry are golden, about 15 minutes. Serve warm.

Serves 4

Lentil Soup

2 tablespoons olive oil
1 large yellow onion, diced
1 teaspoon ground cumin
1 large or 2 small carrots, peeled
   and diced
2 cups (14 oz/440 g) lentils
5–6 cups (40–48 fl oz/1.25–1.5 l)
   Chicken Stock (*recipe on page 13*)
   or broth
2 cups (4 oz/125 g) coarsely chopped
   spinach or Swiss chard or watercress,
   carefully washed
salt and ground pepper to taste
plain yogurt or crème fraîche (optional)

Brown, red, or green lentils can be used in this soup. The green lentils are firmest, so they are the best choice if you want to see whole lentils in the soup. The soup can be prepared the day before and reheated, but wilt and stir in the greens just before serving. A dollop of yogurt or crème fraîche adds a sharpness that cuts the richness of the lentils.

❧

In a saucepan over medium heat, warm the olive oil. Add the onion and sauté until tender and translucent, about 8 minutes. Add the cumin, carrots, lentils, and stock or broth. The amount of liquid will vary, depending upon how dry the lentils are; older, dryer lentils will require the larger amount. Reduce the heat to low, cover, and simmer until the lentils are soft; begin testing for doneness after 20 minutes.

Meanwhile, in a large sauté pan over medium heat, place the spinach or other greens with just the rinsing water clinging to the leaves. Cook, turning occasionally, just until wilted, about 2 minutes. Transfer to a sieve and drain well, pressing out the excess liquid.

Stir the greens into the lentils. Season with salt and pepper. Serve at once in warmed bowls; top each serving with yogurt or crème fraîche, if desired.

Serves 6

Gravlax with Mustard Sauce

1 whole salmon fillet, 2–3 lb (1–1.5 kg),
   with skin intact
¼ cup (2 oz/60 g) sugar
3 tablespoons kosher salt
½ teaspoon ground pepper
1 tablespoon ground juniper berries
2 teaspoons ground coriander
½ teaspoon ground allspice
zest of 2 small lemons, cut into strips
   2 inches (5 cm) long and ¼ inch
   (6 mm) wide
3 large fresh mint sprigs
3 tablespoons gin

FOR THE MUSTARD SAUCE:
¼ cup (2 oz/60 g) Dijon mustard
1 teaspoon dry mustard
3 tablespoons sugar
2 tablespoons white wine vinegar
½ cup (4 fl oz/125 ml) peanut oil
3 tablespoons chopped fresh mint

1 large English (hothouse) cucumber,
   peeled, halved lengthwise, seeded, and
   thinly sliced
thinly sliced pumpernickel bread

It is too difficult to cure a small piece of fish and then slice it neatly. Therefore, it is best to use a 2–3-pound (1–1.5-kg) whole salmon fillet and have some leftovers for a first course for another occasion. Using gin and mint creates a particularly light and delicate gravlax with a bold pink color. If you like, substitute aquavit for the gin and the mint for a more traditional gravlax.

❧

*P*lace the fish fillet, skin side down, in a glass or plastic container. In a small bowl, stir together the sugar, salt, pepper, juniper, coriander, and allspice. Rub this mixture evenly onto the flesh side of the fish. Cover the fish with the lemon zest strips and the mint. Sprinkle with the gin.

Cover the fish with plastic wrap. Place a board or tray directly on the fish and then weight the fish with 2 bricks or other heavy weights. Refrigerate for 4 or 5 days, basting the fish daily with the juices that accumulate. Remove the weights on the last day.

To make the sauce, in a food processor or blender, combine the Dijon mustard, dry mustard, sugar, and vinegar. Pulse just to combine. With the motor running, slowly add the peanut oil in a thin, steady stream, processing until the mixture thickens. Transfer to a small bowl. Fold in the mint. (The sauce can be made up to 1 day in advance, covered, and refrigerated until serving.)

To serve, uncover the gravlax and discard the zest strips and mint sprigs. Slice the gravlax across the grain at an angle and away from the skin into paper-thin slices. Arrange on a serving platter or individual plates with the cucumber and pumpernickel. Pass the mustard sauce at the table.

Serves 6

Deviled Crab Cakes with Ginger-Citrus Vinaigrette

FOR THE CRAB CAKES:
3 tablespoons unsalted butter
1 cup (5 oz/155 g) minced yellow onion
⅓ cup (1½ oz/45 g) minced celery
¼ cup (1½ oz/45 g) finely chopped red or green bell pepper (capsicum)
1 tablespoon dry mustard
½ teaspoon cayenne pepper
1 lb (500 g) fresh crabmeat, picked over
⅓ cup (3 fl oz/80 ml) mayonnaise
1 egg, lightly beaten
½ cup (1 oz/30 g) fresh bread crumbs
1 tablespoon grated lemon zest
¼ cup (⅓ oz/10 g) chopped fresh flat-leaf (Italian) parsley
salt and ground black pepper to taste
1 cup (4 oz/125 g) fine dried bread crumbs

FOR THE GINGER-CITRUS VINAIGRETTE:
¾ cup (6 fl oz/180 ml) peanut oil
finely grated zest of 1 lemon or lime
¼ cup (2 fl oz/60 ml) lemon or lime juice
2 tablespoons peeled and grated fresh ginger
1 jalapeño chile, seeded and minced
sugar and salt to taste

8 cups mixed torn lettuces
peanut oil for frying

Watercress can be used for part of the lettuce, and the greens can be garnished with diced avocado or mango before drizzling with the vinaigrette.

❧

*T*o make the crab cakes, in a sauté pan over medium heat, melt the butter. Add the onion and sauté until translucent, 8–10 minutes. Add the celery and bell pepper and sauté until tender, about 5 minutes longer. Stir in the mustard and cayenne pepper and cook for 1–2 minutes, stirring constantly. Transfer to a bowl and let cool completely. Add the crabmeat, mayonnaise, egg, fresh bread crumbs, lemon zest, and parsley. Fold together without overmixing. Season with salt and black pepper. Form into 8 cakes each about ½ inch (12 mm) thick.

Place the dried bread crumbs on a plate and, working with 1 cake at a time, coat the cakes evenly with the crumbs. Cover and refrigerate for at least 1 hour or as long as overnight.

To make the vinaigrette, in a bowl, whisk together the peanut oil, lemon or lime zest and juice, ginger, and jalapeño. Season with sugar and salt. Toss the lettuces with half of the vinaigrette and divide among 4–8 individual plates.

To cook the crab cakes, in a large frying pan over medium-high heat, pour in oil to a depth of 1 inch (2.5 cm). When the oil is shimmery, slip the cakes into the pan, working in batches if the pan is too crowded. Fry, turning once, until golden, 2–3 minutes on each side.

Place the warm crab cakes atop the greens and drizzle with the remaining vinaigrette. Serve at once.

Serves 4–8

Roasted Eggplant with Pita

3 large eggplants (aubergines)
⅔ cup (3 oz/90 g) almonds
1 cup (8 oz/250 g) plain nonfat yogurt
2 tablespoons lemon juice, or to taste
1 tablespoon minced garlic
1 teaspoon minced jalapeño chile, or
   more to taste
2 teaspoons ground cumin
salt and ground pepper to taste
¼ cup (⅓ oz/10 g) chopped fresh mint
4 pita bread rounds, each cut into
   6 wedges

If you make this low-fat dish ahead of time, wait until just before serving to fold in the mint and almonds. The recipe can easily be halved to serve 6; use 2 medium eggplants instead of 3 large ones.

Preheat an oven to 400°F (200°C). Place the eggplants on a baking sheet and prick all over with a fork. Roast, turning occasionally for even cooking, until the eggplants are soft and tender, about 1 hour. Remove from the oven and let sit until cool enough to handle. Peel the eggplants and place the pulp in a colander to drain for about 30 minutes.

Reduce the oven temperature to 350°F (180°C). Spread the almonds on a baking sheet and toast until lightly colored and fragrant, 5–7 minutes. Remove from the oven, let cool, and chop; set aside.

Place the eggplant pulp in a food processor or blender and pulse to purée. Add the yogurt, lemon juice, garlic, jalapeño, and cumin. Pulse briefly to mix. Add the salt and pepper.

Transfer the purée to a serving bowl. (If desired, cover and refrigerate for up to 6 hours.) Stir in the chopped almonds and mint. Serve with the pita wedges.

Serves 12

Blue Cheese Spread with Walnuts

1 lb (500 g) soft white cheese such as cream cheese or ricotta cheese, at room temperature

5 oz (150 g) blue cheese such as Roquefort or Gorgonzola, at room temperature

1 tablespoon cognac or Armagnac

salt and ground pepper to taste

12 walnut halves, finely chopped

1 bunch fresh chives, snipped

Walnuts and blue cheese—whether Roquefort, Gorgonzola, Stilton, or another variety—are a favorite European pairing. Accompany the spread with crostini (page 13), breadsticks, or fresh vegetables.

❧

In a bowl, combine the white and blue cheeses and mash together with a fork until smooth. Stir in the cognac or Armagnac and a little salt and pepper.

When the mixture is smooth, add the walnuts and chives. Mix again until well blended. Spoon into a serving bowl.

Serves 8

Cold Cucumber Soup

2 tablespoons unsalted butter

1 yellow onion, diced

3–4 cups (24–32 fl oz/750 ml–1 l)
   Chicken Stock (recipe on page 13)
   or broth

1 small potato, about 4 oz (125 g),
   peeled and diced

3 cucumbers, peeled, seeded, and diced

1 cup (8 oz/250 g) plain yogurt or ½ cup
   (4 fl oz/125 ml) heavy (double) cream

salt and ground pepper to taste

3 tablespoons chopped fresh dill or mint
   or basil

In this ideal soup for a hot summer day, mint, dill, or basil is a refreshing garnish. Or for added crunch, garnish with cucumber slices or chopped toasted walnuts, pine nuts, or almonds. Prepare the soup the day before and chill well. Adjust the seasonings at serving time.

❧

*I*n a saucepan over medium heat, melt the butter. Add the onion and sauté until tender and translucent, 8–10 minutes. Add 3 cups (24 fl oz/750 ml) of the stock or broth and the potato, raise the heat to high, and bring to a boil. Reduce the heat to medium and simmer, uncovered, for 10 minutes. Add the cucumbers and continue to simmer until the cucumbers are soft, about 10 minutes longer.

Working in batches, transfer to a food processor or to a blender and purée until smooth. If the purée is too thick, add as much of the remaining 1 cup (8 fl oz/250 ml) stock or broth as needed to thin to a soup consistency. Transfer to a bowl, let cool slightly, and then whisk in the yogurt or cream. Cover and refrigerate the soup until well chilled, at least 3 hours or as long as overnight.

Season with salt and pepper and ladle into chilled bowls. Garnish with herb of choice and serve.

Serves 6

Marinated Button Mushrooms

⅔ cup (5 fl oz/160 ml) dry white wine

⅔ cup (5 fl oz/160 ml) rice vinegar

1 small red bell pepper (capsicum), seeded and cut into ⅜-inch (1-cm) squares

1 lemon, thinly sliced, seeded, and slices cut into quarters

2 tablespoons snipped fresh parsley

2 teaspoons dried oregano

3 whole cloves

1 clove garlic

1 dried hot chile, crumbled

1 teaspoon fine sea salt

1 teaspoon coarsely ground pepper

1 lb (500 g) very small button mushrooms, brushed clean

3 tablespoons extra-virgin olive oil

Rice vinegar, chile, and cloves contribute to the spicy-sweet taste these young, tender mushrooms take on during marinating. You can keep the mushrooms in the refrigerator for up to 5 days; they will only gain in flavor. Snipped fresh cilantro (coriander) can replace the parsley, in which case 1 tablespoon coriander seeds should be added to the marinade.

❧

*I*n a large nonaluminum saucepan, combine the wine, vinegar, bell pepper, lemon, parsley, oregano, cloves, garlic, chile, salt, and ground pepper. Bring to a boil and add the mushrooms. Sprinkle the olive oil over the top and boil for 7 minutes. Remove from the heat and let cool completely before serving.

Serve the mushrooms at room temperature, divided among individual plates or arranged on a platter and accompanied with toothpicks.

Serves 4–6

Beef Meatballs with Parmesan

1½ lb (750 g) lean ground (minced) beef
salt and ground pepper to taste
4 pinches of ground nutmeg
½ cup (2 oz/60 g) grated Parmesan
   cheese
¼ cup (¾ oz/20 g) minced fresh parsley
4 tablespoons (2 fl oz/ 60 ml) extra-virgin
   olive oil

If you've ever wondered why Italian meatballs have so much flavor, one of the secrets—revealed here—is the addition of Parmesan cheese. You can substitute pork or veal for part or all of the beef.

In a bowl, combine the beef, salt, and pepper. Add the nutmeg, Parmesan cheese, and parsley, and knead with your hands until thoroughly mixed.

Rub nuggets of the meat mixture between your palms to form balls the size of walnuts. Dampen your hands with cold water to make the shaping easier.

In a large nonstick frying pan over medium heat, warm 2 tablespoons of the olive oil. Arrange half the meatballs in the pan and cook until golden brown, about 5 minutes. Every now and again, rotate the pan in a smooth, circular motion so that the balls will turn to cook on all sides. Using a slotted spoon, transfer the meatballs to a serving plate. Add the remaining 2 tablespoons oil to the pan and cook the remaining meatballs in the same manner.

Serve the meatballs hot, warm, or at room temperature with toothpicks or skewers.

Serves 6–8

Asian-Inspired Shrimp Salad with Tropical Fruit

4 cups (32 fl oz/1 l) water or dry
    white wine
1 lb (500 g) shrimp (prawns), peeled and
    deveined (about 20)
2 ripe papayas or mangoes
6 cups (12 oz/375 g) torn mixed lettuces
6 tablespoons (½ oz/15 g) torn fresh mint
    leaves
6 tablespoons (½ oz/15 g) torn fresh basil
    leaves

FOR THE VINAIGRETTE:
⅔ cup (5 fl oz/160 ml) peanut oil or
    olive oil
grated zest of 2 limes
6 tablespoons (3 fl oz/90 ml) lime juice
2 tablespoons brown sugar
1 teaspoon red pepper flakes or
    1 teaspoon diced jalapeño chile, or
    to taste
salt to taste

Tangy fruit and opalescent pink shrimp dressed with a spicy sweet-and-tart vinaigrette make a nice light beginning for a special meal. If you cannot find papayas or mangoes in the market, 4 oranges, peeled and sectioned, or 1 cantaloupe, peeled, seeded, and diced, can be substituted. If you like, poach the shrimp the night before or earlier in the day and then assemble the salad at the last minute.

✳

*I*n a saucepan over high heat, bring the water or wine to a boil. Add the shrimp and cook until they turn pink and curl, 3–5 minutes. Using a slotted spoon, transfer to a bowl. Cover and refrigerate until needed.

If using papayas, peel, then cut in half lengthwise and scoop out and discard the seeds. Dice or slice the flesh. If using mangoes, cut off the flesh from either side of the large central pit, then peel and dice or slice the flesh.

In a bowl combine the lettuces, mint, and basil and toss to mix.

To make the vinaigrette, in a small bowl, thoroughly whisk together the peanut or olive oil, lime zest and juice, brown sugar, pepper flakes or jalapeño pepper, and salt.

Add a few tablespoons of the vinaigrette to the shrimp, toss well, and let stand for a few minutes. Drizzle half of the remaining vinaigrette over the lettuces and herbs and toss thoroughly. Divide the lettuce mixture among 4 individual plates. Top with the shrimp and papaya or mango. Drizzle the remaining vinaigrette over the top.

Serves 4

Tomato Salad with Basil-Honey Vinaigrette

FOR THE VINAIGRETTE:
3–4 tablespoons balsamic vinegar
　(see note)
3 tablespoons full-flavored honey
1 teaspoon salt
¾ cup (6 fl oz/180 ml) olive oil
½ cup (¾ oz/20 g) tightly packed
　chopped fresh basil

2–2½ lb (1–1.25 kg) ripe beefsteak or
　other flavorful tomatoes

The aromatic vinaigrette also complements avocados and pears or melon. Some balsamic vinegars are sharper than others, so start with 3 tablespoons and add more as needed to taste. Do not use strong olive oil for this recipe or the balance of sweet and sour will be overwhelmed.

✳

To make the vinaigrette, in a small bowl, whisk together the vinegar, honey, and salt. Add the olive oil and basil and whisk to blend well. Taste and adjust the seasonings.

Slice the tomatoes and arrange on a platter. Drizzle the vinaigrette over the tomatoes and serve.

Serves 6

Asparagus with Toasted Almonds and Balsamic Vinaigrette

¾ cup (3 oz/90 g) slivered blanched
   almonds or pine nuts
2 lb (1 kg) fresh asparagus
¼ cup (2 oz/60 g) unsalted butter
¼ cup (2 fl oz/60 ml) olive oil
⅓ cup (3 fl oz/80 ml) balsamic vinegar,
   or to taste
salt and ground pepper to taste

You can serve the asparagus either hot or at room temperature, allowing you flexibility in make-ahead preparations.

✳

Preheat an oven to 350°F (180°C). Spread the nuts on a baking sheet and toast until lightly colored and fragrant, 5–7 minutes. Remove from the oven and let cool.

Remove the tough ends of the asparagus spears. If the stalks are thick, using a vegetable peeler or paring knife and starting about 2 inches (5 cm) below the tip, peel off the outer skin.

Half fill a large, wide frying pan with salted water and bring to a boil. Add the asparagus spears and boil until tender-crisp, 4–6 minutes; the timing will depend upon the thickness of the stalks. Drain well and pat dry. Arrange on a serving platter and keep warm.

In a large sauté pan over medium heat, melt the butter with the olive oil. Add the nuts and stir until hot. Add the balsamic vinegar and, when bubbly, pour over the asparagus. Season with salt and pepper and serve.

Serves 6

Glazed Carrots with Grapes and Walnuts

1 large bunch carrots, peeled and thinly
   sliced (about 6 cups/1½ lb/750 g)
¼ cup (2 oz/60 g) unsalted butter
1 cup (8 fl oz/250 ml) Chicken Stock
   (recipe on page 13) or broth
3 tablespoons sugar
1 cup (6 oz/185 g) seedless red grapes,
   cut in half
½ cup (2 oz/60 g) chopped walnuts
salt and ground pepper to taste

The carrots and grapes can be prepared for cooking up to 8 hours in advance. For a citrusy accent, add 2 teaspoons grated lemon or orange zest with the stock or broth. A sprinkling of chopped fresh mint makes a good garnish.

✳

*I*n a wide sauté pan over high heat, combine the carrots, butter, stock or broth, and sugar. Bring to a boil, reduce the heat to medium-low, and simmer, uncovered, until the carrots are tender and the pan juices are reduced to a syrupy glaze, 8–10 minutes.

   Stir in the grapes and walnuts and season with salt and pepper. Transfer to a warmed serving dish and serve immediately.

Serves 6–8

Green Salad with Cucumbers, Walnuts, and Mustard-Shallot Vinaigrette

1½ cups (6 oz/185 g) walnuts
9 cups (9 oz/280 g) mixed torn salad
   greens, including romaine (cos) and
   butter lettuces and watercress
2 cucumbers, peeled, seeded, and diced
3 tablespoons chopped fresh dill
   (optional)

FOR THE MUSTARD-SHALLOT VINAIGRETTE:
2 tablespoons Dijon mustard
3 tablespoons red wine vinegar
½ cup (4 fl oz/125 ml) mild olive oil
¼ cup (1¼ oz/37 g) minced shallots
salt and ground pepper to taste

This full-flavored vinaigrette coats the salad greens and adds a little zip to the crunchy cucumbers. You can make the vinaigrette early in the day and toast the walnuts and wash and crisp the greens a few hours ahead. Then just toss and serve.

✳

Preheat an oven to 350°F (180°C). Spread the walnuts on a baking sheet and toast until lightly colored and fragrant, 5–7 minutes. Remove from the oven and let cool.

In a large salad bowl, combine the salad greens, cucumbers, walnuts, and dill, if using.

To make the vinaigrette, in a small bowl, whisk together the mustard and vinegar. Gradually whisk in the olive oil until well blended. Stir in the shallots and season with salt and pepper.

Drizzle the vinaigrette over the salad, toss well, and serve.

Serves 6

41

Potato and Onion Gratin

2 teaspoons minced garlic
2 lb (1 kg) baking potatoes, peeled and
 thinly sliced
salt and ground pepper to taste
ground nutmeg to taste
1 white sweet onion, halved lengthwise
 and each half thinly sliced lengthwise
1 cup (8 fl oz/250 ml) milk
1 cup (8 fl oz/250 ml) heavy (double)
 cream

The potatoes should be sliced to a uniform thickness so they cook evenly. A mandoline is a good tool for this step. Make sure the baking dish you choose is large enough for the top of the potatoes to be well below the rim; otherwise, the milk and cream may bubble over.

✳

Preheat an oven to 375° F (190° C). Butter a 1½- or 2-qt (1.5- or 2-l) rectangular or oval baking dish.

Sprinkle the garlic over the bottom of the prepared dish. Layer half of the potato slices, in overlapping rows, over the garlic. Sprinkle lightly with salt, pepper, and nutmeg. Spread the onion slices evenly over the potatoes, then layer the remaining potato slices over the top, arranging them attractively. Carefully pour the milk over the potatoes, moistening all of the potato slices as you do. Then pour ½ cup (4 fl oz/125 ml) of the cream over the potato slices, also being careful to moisten all of the slices. Sprinkle to taste with salt, pepper, and nutmeg.

Bake until the potatoes are very tender when pierced and golden brown on top and have absorbed most of the milk and cream, 1–1½ hours. During the first 40 minutes of baking, baste the potatoes every 10 minutes by tipping the dish a little and scooping up the liquid with a large spoon. Be sure to baste all of the potato slices so that an even golden coating forms. During the last 20–40 minutes of baking, baste the potatoes every 10 minutes with the remaining ½ cup (4 fl oz/125 ml) cream, again being sure to coat all of the slices. You may not need all of the cream.

Remove from the oven and serve hot directly from the dish.

Serves 4

Broccoli and Olives with Garlic and Pepper Vinaigrette

1 large or 2 small heads broccoli, about 1½ lb (750 g) total weight, cut into florets with stems intact and thick stems peeled
½ cup (4 fl oz/125 ml) olive oil
2 teaspoons red pepper flakes
2 tablespoons red wine vinegar
2 cloves garlic, minced
salt and ground pepper to taste
1 cup (5 oz/155 g) Gaeta or similar black olives

The spicy-hot vinaigrette is also good on cooked cauliflower or zucchini (courgettes). It can be made 4–6 hours in advance of combining with the broccoli. The broccoli can be cooked and chilled 2–4 hours before serving.

✳

*B*ring a large pot three-fourths full of salted water to a boil. Add the broccoli and cook until tender-crisp, 3–4 minutes. Drain, being careful not to break the florets, and immediately immerse in ice water to stop the cooking and preserve the vibrant color. Drain well again and pat dry with paper towels. Cover and chill well.

In a small saucepan over medium heat, warm the olive oil until it is very hot but not smoking. Drop in the pepper flakes and heat until the oil is red, about 30 seconds. Remove from the heat and let cool. Strain through a fine-mesh sieve into a measuring cup. Stir in the vinegar and garlic; season with salt and ground pepper.

Just before serving, arrange the chilled broccoli on a platter. Drizzle with the vinaigrette and sprinkle with the olives. Serve immediately.

Serves 4

Escarole Salad with Pear and Prosciutto

1 large head escarole, torn into bite-sized
   pieces
leaves from 3 or 4 fresh tarragon sprigs,
   chopped
1 tablespoon lemon juice, plus juice of
   1 lemon
⅛ teaspoon salt
1 teaspoon Dijon mustard
ground pepper to taste
¼ cup (2 fl oz/60 ml) extra-virgin
   olive oil
2 ripe but firm pears, preferably Comice
   (see note)
16 thin, lean prosciutto slices
¾ cup (4½ oz/140 g) seedless red grapes,
   cut in half if large

Comice pears are the best choice to serve with prosciutto. You can, however, substitute red Bartlett (Williams') or Anjou pears. If escarole is unavailable, substitute chicory (curly endive), oak-leaf lettuce, or some other flavorful lettuce variety. If you cannot find fresh tarragon, use fresh mint.

✳

In a bowl, combine the escarole and tarragon and toss to mix. Cover with a damp towel and refrigerate to crisp.

In a small bowl, whisk together the 1 tablespoon lemon juice and the salt until the salt dissolves. Stir in the mustard and season with pepper, then whisk in the olive oil until well blended. Taste and adjust the seasonings. Set aside.

Place the juice of 1 lemon in a large bowl. Cut the pears into quarters, remove the stems and cores, and then cut each quarter into 2 wedges. Place the pear wedges in the bowl with the lemon juice and toss carefully to coat all cut surfaces.

Carefully separate the prosciutto slices and then wrap a slice around each pear wedge.

Whisk the dressing again and pour it over the greens. Toss to mix well. Divide the greens among individual plates. Scatter the grapes over the greens. Arrange 4 prosciutto-wrapped pear wedges on each plate. Serve at once.

Serves 4

Moroccan Vegetables

¼ cup (1½ oz/45 g) almonds (optional)

2 tablespoons olive oil

1 large yellow onion, diced

2 cloves garlic, minced

½ teaspoon salt

1 teaspoon ground ginger

1 teaspoon paprika

½ teaspoon ground black pepper

½ teaspoon cayenne pepper, or to taste

½ teaspoon ground cinnamon

1 cup (8 fl oz/250 ml) Chicken Stock
   (*recipe on page 13*) or broth

6 carrots, peeled and cut crosswise into
   2-inch (5-cm) lengths

1 large cauliflower, cut into florets

2 tablespoons lemon juice

¼ cup (⅓ oz/10 g) chopped fresh mint

Moroccan, Kalamata, Sicilian, or other
   full-flavored black olives (optional)

Despite the numerous ingredients that go into this dish, it is actually quite easy to prepare and serve. Both the carrots and the cauliflower can be parboiled and the seasoned onion prepared the night before. Then all you need to do before serving is reheat the onion and add the vegetables and seasonings.

✳

*I*f using almonds, preheat an oven to 350°F (180°C). Spread the almonds on a baking sheet and toast until lightly colored and fragrant, 5–7 minutes. Remove from the oven and set aside to cool.

In a large sauté pan over medium heat, warm the olive oil. Add the onion and sauté until tender and translucent, 8–10 minutes. Add the garlic, salt, ginger, paprika, black pepper, cayenne pepper, and cinnamon and sauté, stirring occasionally, for 3 minutes longer. Add the stock or broth and simmer for 1–2 minutes. Remove from the heat and set aside in the pan.

Bring a saucepan three-fourths full of salted water to a boil. Add the carrots and boil until tender but still firm, 5–6 minutes. Using a slotted spoon, transfer the carrots to a bowl. Add the cauliflower florets to the same boiling water and boil until tender but still firm, about 5 minutes. Drain well.

Reheat the onion mixture over medium heat. Add the carrots and cauliflower and toss well to coat with the onion mixture. When the mixture reaches a simmer, cover and heat until warmed to serving temperature. Stir in the lemon juice, then taste and adjust the seasonings.

To serve, transfer to a serving dish and sprinkle with the mint and with the olives and almonds, if using.

Serves 6

Yam Gratin

¼ cup (1½ oz/45 g) hazelnuts (filberts)
   (optional)
6–8 yams, about 3 lb (1.5 kg) total
   weight
½ cup (4 fl oz/125 ml) apple cider
¼ cup (2 fl oz/60 ml) maple syrup
¼ cup (2 oz/60 g) firmly packed
   brown sugar
1 tablespoon lemon juice
½ teaspoon ground ginger or nutmeg
½ teaspoon ground cinnamon
6 tablespoons (3 oz/90 g) unsalted butter
salt to taste

This delicious cream-free gratin is made with what Americans call yams, although these dark-skinned tubers with deep orange flesh are actually a variety of sweet potato and unrelated to the true yam. The gratin can be assembled about 4 hours before serving.

✳

*I*f using the hazelnuts, preheat an oven to 350°F (180°C). Spread the hazelnuts on a baking sheet and toast until lightly colored and fragrant, and the skins split and loosen, 5–10 minutes. Remove from the oven, let cool, then wrap in a clean kitchen towel. Rub against them with your palms to remove most of the skins. Chop the nuts coarsely and set aside.

Raise the oven temperature to 375°F (190°C). Butter a large rectangular baking dish.

Bring a large saucepan three-fourths full of water to a boil. Add the yams and boil, uncovered, until they can be pierced but are still quite firm, about 30 minutes. Drain, immerse in cool water, and drain again. Peel the yams and slice crosswise ½ inch (12 mm) thick. Arrange the slices in a single layer, overlapping them, in the prepared baking dish.

Meanwhile, in a small saucepan over medium heat, combine the apple cider, maple syrup, brown sugar, lemon juice, ginger or nutmeg, and cinnamon. Bring to a boil, stirring to dissolve the sugar, and boil for 10 minutes. Swirl in the butter, then pour the mixture evenly over the yams. Sprinkle lightly with salt and strew the toasted hazelnuts, if using, over the top.

Bake uncovered, basting occasionally with the pan juices, until the yams are tender when pierced, 20–25 minutes. Serve hot directly from the dish.

Serves 6

Insalata Capricciosa

FOR THE GARLIC VINAIGRETTE:

⅔ cup (5 fl oz/160 ml) pure olive oil

⅓ cup (3 fl oz/80 ml) extra-virgin
  olive oil

¼ cup (2 fl oz/60 ml) red wine vinegar

1 tablespoon balsamic vinegar (optional)

2 teaspoons minced garlic

salt and ground pepper to taste

1½–2 cups (10½–14 oz/330–440 g)
  drained, cooked chickpeas (garbanzo
  beans)

1 small head cauliflower, cut into florets
  (optional)

12 cups (1½ lb/750 g) torn romaine (cos)
  lettuce

2 cups (10 oz/315 g) peeled, seeded, and
  diced English (hothouse) cucumber

1 cup (4 oz/125 g) thinly sliced carrot

Capricciosa more or less means "with whimsy," so use your imagination when putting this salad together. Start with romaine and then add whatever you like in addition to or in place of what appears here, such as a few olives or a handful of croutons. You can use canned chickpeas in place of homecooked, in which case you should rinse and drain them well before mixing with the vinaigrette.

✳

*T*o make the vinaigrette, in a small bowl, whisk together the pure and extra-virgin olive oils, wine vinegar, balsamic vinegar (if using), and garlic. Season with salt and pepper and set aside.

Place the chickpeas in a bowl and add ½ cup (4 fl oz/125 ml) of the vinaigrette. Stir to coat the chickpeas well and let marinate for 12 hours. Set the remaining vinaigrette aside.

If using the cauliflower florets, bring a saucepan three-fourths full of water to a boil. Add the florets and boil until tender-crisp, 3–5 minutes. Drain well and immerse in ice water to stop the cooking and cool completely. Drain well again and pat dry with paper towels.

In a large salad bowl, combine the lettuce, cucumber, carrot, chickpeas, and cauliflower, if using. Drizzle the remaining vinaigrette over the top, toss well, and serve.

Serves 6

Rice Pilaf with Dried Apricots, Slivered Almonds, and Mint

½ cup (2 oz/60 g) slivered almonds

1 tablespoon olive oil

1 tablespoon unsalted butter

2 shallots, minced

1½ cups (10½ oz/330 g) long-grain
white rice

3 cups (24 fl oz/750 ml) Chicken Stock
(*recipe on page 13*) or broth

½ cup (3 oz/90 g) dried apricot halves,
slivered

¾ teaspoon salt

3 tablespoons julienned fresh mint leaves

The combination of savory, sweet, tart, and earthy flavors in this simple pilaf gives it a marvelous versatility, making it an equally good partner for European, Mediterranean, Middle Eastern, or Indian main courses. Feel free to vary the formula, substituting other dried fruits, nuts, or fresh herbs.

✳

Preheat an oven to 350° F (180° C). Spread the nuts on a baking sheet and toast until lightly colored and fragrant, 5–7 minutes. Remove from the oven and let cool.

In a saucepan over medium-low heat, warm the olive oil and butter until the butter melts. Add the shallots and sauté, stirring, until lightly golden, about 5 minutes.

Meanwhile, put the rice in a fine-mesh sieve, rinse well with cold running water, and drain. When the shallots are ready, add the rice and stir briefly to coat the grains with the oil and butter.

Stir in the stock or broth, apricots, and salt. Raise the heat and bring to a boil; then reduce the heat to very low, cover, and simmer undisturbed for 20 minutes. Remove the rice from the heat and uncover to check if it is tender and all the liquid has been absorbed; if not, cover the pan again and cook for a few minutes longer.

Add the toasted almonds and half of the mint to the rice and toss lightly with a fork to distribute evenly. Transfer to a warmed serving dish and strew the remaining mint on top.

Serves 6

Pork Loin with Pomegranate and Orange Glaze

1 boneless pork loin, about 3 lb (1.5 kg), tied for roasting, or 3 pork tenderloins, about 1 lb (500 g) each

FOR THE SPICE PASTE:
2 teaspoons minced garlic
2 tablespoons Dijon mustard
grated zest of 1 orange
⅓ cup (3 fl oz/80 ml) orange juice
2 tablespoons peeled and grated fresh ginger
2 tablespoons pomegranate syrup
2 tablespoons soy sauce

FOR THE BASTING SAUCE:
⅓ cup (3 fl oz/80 ml) orange juice
3 tablespoons honey
3 tablespoons pomegranate syrup
2 tablespoons soy sauce

Pomegranate syrup, a concentrate made from pomegranate juice, is available in specialty markets. If the syrup is unavailable, fresh or bottled pomegranate juice can be reduced over high heat to a syrupy consistency. Marinate the pork in the spice paste overnight for the fullest flavor. The tenderloins can also be cooked in a broiler (griller).

Place the pork in a nonaluminum dish. To make the spice paste, in a bowl, combine the garlic, mustard, orange zest and juice, ginger, pomegranate syrup, and soy sauce. Rub onto the meat, cover, and refrigerate for at least 6 hours or up to overnight. Bring to room temperature before grilling.

Prepare a fire in a grill.

To make the basting sauce, in a small bowl, stir together the orange juice, honey, pomegranate syrup, and soy sauce.

Place the pork loin or tenderloins on an oiled grill rack not too close to the heat source. Grill, brushing with the basting sauce and turning often until nicely glazed, 15–20 minutes on each side for the large loin and 5 minutes per side for the smaller tenderloins for medium, or until an instant-read thermometer inserted into the center registers 140°F (60°C) or the meat is pale pink when cut with a sharp knife.

Transfer the pork to a work surface, cover loosely with aluminum foil, and let rest for 8–10 minutes. Snip the strings if tied and thinly slice across the grain. Serve at once.

Serves 6

Seafood Chowder

3 tablespoons olive oil

2 yellow onions, chopped

3 cloves garlic, minced

1 tablespoon peeled and grated fresh
   ginger

grated zest of 1 lime or lemon

1 tablespoon paprika

3 celery stalks, chopped

4 tomatoes, peeled, seeded, and diced

2 jalapeño chiles, seeded, if desired, and
   minced

6 cups (48 fl oz/1.5 l) fish broth or
   Chicken Stock (recipe on page 13)
   or broth

2 cups (10 oz/315 g) diced, peeled
   potatoes

1 cup (6 oz/185 g) corn kernels (fresh or
   thawed frozen)

1 cup (5 oz/155 g) baby lima beans (fresh
   or thawed frozen)

1 cup (8 fl oz/250 ml) half-and-half (half
   cream) or heavy (double) cream
   (optional)

2 lb (1 kg) assorted firm white fish fillets,
   cut into spoon-sized chunks, or a
   mixture of fish fillets and shellfish

salt and ground pepper to taste

3 tablespoons chopped fresh cilantro
   (fresh coriander)

For this Latin American–inspired chowder, use firm, white-fleshed fish, such as cod, snapper, halibut, angler, flounder, or sea bass. A variety of shellfish can also be added, including shelled clams, shrimp (prawns), and scallops.

❦

*I*n a large, deep saucepan over medium heat, warm the olive oil. Add the onions and sauté, stirring, until tender and translucent, 8–10 minutes. Add the garlic, ginger, lime or lemon zest, and paprika and sauté for 2 minutes. Then add the celery, tomatoes, and jalapeños and sauté for 2 minutes longer.

Add the broth or stock and the potatoes and bring to a boil. Reduce the heat to medium and simmer, uncovered, until the potatoes are about half-cooked, 10–12 minutes.

Add the corn, lima beans, half-and-half or cream (if using), and fish or fish and shellfish and simmer, uncovered, until just cooked, about 5 minutes; do not overcook or the seafood will toughen. Season with salt and pepper.

Ladle into warmed bowls and sprinkle with the cilantro. Serve immediately.

Serves 6

Roasted Rosemary Chicken

1 chicken, 3½–4½ lb (1.75–2.25 kg),
    giblets and neck discarded or reserved
    for another use
1 lemon, quartered
salt to taste
3 cloves garlic, smashed
7 fresh rosemary sprigs
extra-virgin olive oil
ground pepper to taste
2 cups (16 fl oz/500 ml) water

*P*reheat an oven to 425°F (220°C).

Remove any fat from around the cavity of the chicken. Rinse the chicken inside and out. Dry with paper towels. Rub the cavity with 1 of the lemon quarters and leave it in the cavity. Sprinkle the cavity lightly with salt. Place the garlic cloves, the remaining 3 lemon quarters, and 3 of the rosemary sprigs in the cavity.

Place one of the remaining rosemary sprigs under each wing and one between each leg and the body of the chicken. Truss the chicken: using kitchen string, tie the legs together and then tie the legs and wings close to the body. Brush the chicken with olive oil and sprinkle with salt and pepper.

Oil a rack in a roasting pan and place the chicken, on its side, on the rack. Add 1 cup (8 fl oz/250 ml) of the water to the pan. Roast for 20 minutes. Turn the chicken onto its other side, brush with olive oil, and roast for another 20 minutes. Turn the chicken breast side up, brush with oil again, and roast for another 10–20 minutes, basting a couple of times with the pan juices. Check if the chicken is done by inserting an instant-read thermometer into the thickest part of the breast or thigh away from the bone. It should register about 165°F (74°C) in the breast or 180°F (82°C) in the thigh. Alternatively, pierce the thigh joint with a knife tip; the juices should run clear. Transfer to a warmed serving platter and cover loosely with aluminum foil. Let rest for 10 minutes before carving.

Using a spoon, skim the fat from the pan juices and discard. Place the pan over medium heat. Add the remaining 1 cup (8 fl oz/250 ml) water to the pan and heat, stirring to dislodge any browned bits from the pan bottom. Simmer for 1–2 minutes, continuing to stir. Season with salt and pepper.

Carve the chicken and arrange on individual plates. Spoon some of the juices over each serving.

Serves 4

Pappardelle with Mushroom Sauce

3 tablespoons unsalted butter

3 tablespoons olive oil

½ lb (250 g) pancetta, sliced ¼ inch (6 mm) thick, then cut into long strips ¼ inch (6 mm) wide (optional)

3 yellow onions, thinly sliced

2 lb (1 kg) mixed fresh mushrooms such as chanterelles, cremini, porcini, portobellos, or shiitakes, cut into slices ¼ inch (6 mm) thick or left whole or halved if small

about ½ cup (4 fl oz/125 ml) beef broth or vegetable broth, if needed

2 tablespoons chopped fresh sage or thyme

1½ tablespoons minced garlic

salt and ground pepper to taste

1½ lb (750 g) fresh pappardelle or fettuccine

grated Parmesan cheese

Nothing is quite so satisfying as a bowl of steaming pasta cloaked in a delectable sauce. Purchase good-quality fresh pappardelle or buy fresh pasta sheets and cut them in strips about 1 inch (2.5 cm) wide. If you prefer a narrower noodle, use fresh fettuccine. The sauce can be made up to 1 hour before serving and then reheated while you cook the pasta.

In a large sauté pan over medium heat, warm 1 tablespoon each of the butter and olive oil. If using the pancetta, add it to the pan and sauté, stirring occasionally, until lightly browned, 2–3 minutes. Add the onions and sauté, stirring occasionally, until almost tender, 7–8 minutes longer. Transfer to a bowl and set aside.

Add 1 tablespoon each butter and olive oil to the same pan over high heat. When the butter melts and is hot, add half of the mushrooms and sauté just until they begin to release their liquid and soften; the timing will depend upon the variety of mushrooms. Transfer to the bowl holding the onions.

Warm the remaining 1 tablespoon each butter and oil in the same pan. Add the remaining mushrooms and sauté in the same manner. Return the mushroom-onion mixture to the sauté pan and reheat over high heat. If the mixture seems dry, add as much of the stock as needed to moisten it. Then stir in the sage or thyme and the garlic and sauté, stirring often, for 2 minutes. Season to taste with salt and pepper. Keep warm.

Meanwhile, bring a large pot three-fourths full of salted water to a boil. When the sauce is ready, drop the pasta into the boiling water and cook, stirring to separate the strands, until al dente (tender but firm to the bite), 1–2 minutes. Drain and transfer to a warmed serving platter. Add the sauce, toss gently, and serve immediately. Pass the Parmesan cheese at the table.

Serves 4

White Fish with Moroccan Spice Marinade

FOR THE MARINADE:

2 tablespoons lemon juice

¼ teaspoon saffron threads, steeped in 3 tablespoons warm water for 30 minutes

3 tablespoons chopped fresh flat-leaf (Italian) parsley

3 tablespoons chopped fresh cilantro (fresh coriander)

1 or 2 cloves garlic, minced

2 teaspoons ground cumin

1½ teaspoons paprika

1 teaspoon salt

1 teaspoon ground pepper

½ teaspoon ground ginger

⅓ teaspoon ground cinnamon

6 tablespoons (3 fl oz/90 ml) olive oil

4 firm white fish fillets such as cod, flounder, halibut, or swordfish, about 6 oz (185 g) each

olive oil for brushing on fish, if broiling (grilling)

This easy dish goes together quickly to produce a wonderfully fragrant and exotic main course. The marinade can be prepared the night before or in the morning and takes just moments to combine. The fish should marinate for at least 40 minutes, but for no more than 1 hour, before cooking. It can be baked or broiled, as you like.

❦

To make the marinade, in a bowl, mix together the lemon juice, saffron and water, parsley, cilantro, garlic, cumin, paprika, salt, pepper, ginger, and cinnamon. Stir in the olive oil. Arrange the fish fillets in nonaluminum container and spoon half of the marinade over them. Turn the fillets to coat evenly. Cover and marinate in the refrigerator for at least 40 minutes or for up to 1 hour. Reserve the remaining marinade.

Preheat an oven to 450°F (230°C), or preheat a broiler (griller).

If baking the fish, lightly oil a baking dish large enough to accommodate the fish in a single layer. Place the fillets in the dish and bake until opaque at the center when pierced, about 8 minutes.

If broiling, lightly brush the fish fillets on both sides with olive oil and place on a broiler pan. Broil (grill), turning once, until opaque at the center, about 4 minutes on each side.

Serve the fillets with the reserved marinade spooned on top.

Serves 4

Simple Country Paella

3 tablespoons minced garlic

2 tablespoons dried oregano

1 tablespoon coarsely ground pepper

2 teaspoons salt

3–4 tablespoons red wine vinegar

12 tablespoons (6 fl oz/180 ml) olive oil

12 small chicken breast halves or 6 small chicken thighs and 6 small chicken breast halves

¼ cup (2 fl oz/60 ml) dry white wine or water, plus extra wine or water for cooking clams or mussels

½ teaspoon saffron threads

2 large yellow onions, chopped

3–4 cups (18–24 oz/560–750 g) seeded and diced canned plum (Roma) tomatoes

2 cups (14 oz/440 g) short-grain white rice

4–5 cups (32–40 fl oz/1–1.25 l) Chicken Stock (recipe on page 13) or broth

24 shrimp (prawns), peeled and deveined (optional)

1 cup (5 oz/155 g) shelled English peas or tender, young lima beans

36 clams and/or mussels in the shell, well scrubbed and debearded if using mussels

*I*n a small bowl, combine 2 tablespoons of the garlic, oregano, pepper, and salt. Add the vinegar and stir to form a paste. Stir in 6 tablespoons (3 fl oz/90 ml) of the olive oil. Place the chicken pieces in a nonaluminum container. Rub the marinade on the chicken, coating evenly. Cover and refrigerate overnight.

In a small saucepan over low heat, warm the ¼ cup (2 fl oz/ 60 ml) wine or water and remove from the heat. Crush the saffron threads gently and add to the warm liquid. Let stand for 10 minutes.

In a large, deep frying pan over medium-high heat, warm the remaining 6 tablespoons (3 fl oz/90 ml) olive oil. Working in batches, add the chicken and brown quickly on all sides. Remove from the pan and set aside. To the oil remaining in the pan, add the onions and cook over medium heat, stirring often, until tender and translucent, 8–10 minutes. Add the remaining 1 tablespoon garlic and tomatoes and cook, stirring, for 5 minutes.

Add the rice, reduce the heat to low, and stir for 3 minutes. Add the stock or broth (the amount you add will depend on the absorbency of the rice) and the saffron and its soaking liquid, raise the heat to high, and bring to a boil. Reduce the heat to low and simmer, uncovered and without stirring, for 10 minutes. Add the browned chicken and continue to cook, uncovered, until the liquids are absorbed and the rice is tender, about 10 minutes longer, adding the shrimp, if using, and the peas or lima beans during the last 5 minutes.

Meanwhile, in a saucepan, place the clams and/or mussels, discarding any that do not close to the touch. Add wine or water to a depth of 1 inch (2.5 cm). Cover, place over medium-high heat, and cook, shaking the pan occasionally, until the shellfish open, about 5 minutes. Add to the paella 1–2 minutes before it is ready, discarding any that did not open.

Let the paella rest for 10 minutes before serving.

Serves 6

Beef Strudel

3 tablespoons unsalted butter or olive oil, plus ½ cup (4 oz/125 g) unsalted butter, melted
1 large yellow onion, finely chopped
1 teaspoon minced garlic
3 tablespoons chopped fresh parsley
3 tablespoons chopped fresh dill
1 teaspoon dried oregano
1 teaspoon ground cinnamon
½ teaspoon ground allspice or nutmeg
1 lb (500 g) ground (minced) beef
1 egg
¼ cup (1 oz/30 g) fine dried bread crumbs
salt and ground pepper to taste
12 sheets filo pastry (about ½ lb/250 g)

Cut this savory strudel on the bias and serve with a dollop of yogurt or sour cream. The strudel can be made up to 12 hours in advance, covered loosely with aluminum foil, and refrigerated until baked.

❦

In a large frying pan or sauté pan over medium heat, warm the 3 tablespoons butter or oil. Add the onion and sauté until soft, 8–10 minutes. Add the garlic, parsley, dill, oregano, cinnamon, allspice or nutmeg, and beef. Cook until the meat is cooked through, breaking up the beef with a wooden spoon and stirring occasionally, about 10 minutes. Transfer to a bowl and let cool slightly. Stir in the egg and bread crumbs and season with salt and pepper. Let cool for 30 minutes or longer.

Preheat an oven to 350°F (180°C). Butter a baking sheet.

As you work with the filo, keep the unused sheets covered with a lightly dampened kitchen towel to prevent them from drying out. Place 1 filo sheet on a clean, dry surface with a long side facing you. Brush with some of the melted butter. Top with a second sheet, brush with more butter, and top with a third sheet. Repeat until 6 sheets in all have been used. Place half of the meat mixture in a strip along the long edge nearest you, leaving a 1-inch (2.5-cm) border. Fold in the ends and, beginning from the long edge nearest you, roll up like a strudel. Repeat with the remaining sheets and meat mixture to make a second roll.

Place the rolls on the prepared baking sheet. Brush with the remaining melted butter. Bake until golden, about 40 minutes. Cut into slices ½ inch (12 mm) thick and serve hot.

Serves 6

Baked Chicken with Artichokes

10 baby artichokes, about 1 lb (500 g) total weight, trimmed (*see glossary, page 104*) and halved lengthwise

6 tablespoons (3 fl oz/90 ml) lemon juice

1 chicken, 3–3½ lb (1.5–1.75 kg), cut into serving pieces

1 tablespoon unsalted butter

1 tablespoon olive oil

8 fresh sage leaves

2 large shallots, chopped

¼ cup (2 fl oz/60 ml) dry white wine or water

salt and ground pepper to taste

1 lemon

Preheat an oven to 425°F (220°C).

Fill a large saucepan half full of water and bring to a boil. Add the artichokes and 3 tablespoons of the lemon juice, reduce the heat to medium-high, and cook, uncovered, until almost tender when pierced, 5–6 minutes. Drain and set aside.

Trim any excess fat from the chicken pieces. Cut each breast half crosswise into 2 pieces. Discard the chicken back, neck, and giblets (if any) or save for another use. Cut off the wing tips and discard.

In a large sauté pan over medium-high heat, melt the butter with the olive oil. When hot, add the chicken pieces, in batches to avoid crowding, and brown lightly, turning once, 4–5 minutes on each side. Using tongs, transfer to a baking dish, skin side down. Tuck 4 of the sage leaves under the chicken.

Reduce the heat under the sauté pan to medium-low and add the shallots. Sauté gently until translucent, 2–3 minutes. Add the wine or water and deglaze the pan, stirring to dislodge any browned bits from the pan bottom. Bring to a boil and pour over the chicken. Sprinkle with 1½ tablespoons of the lemon juice. Season with salt and pepper.

Bake for 20 minutes, basting several times. Turn the chicken over, skin side up, add the artichoke halves, and continue to bake, basting occasionally, until the chicken and artichokes are tender and the juices run clear when a thigh is pierced, 20–30 minutes longer.

Using tongs or a slotted spoon, transfer the chicken and artichokes to a warmed serving dish. If necessary, place the pan over high heat to thicken the juices. Season with the remaining 1½ tablespoons lemon juice and salt and pepper. Pour the juices over the chicken. Holding the lemon over the serving dish, grate the zest directly onto the chicken pieces. Garnish with the remaining 4 sage leaves.

Serves 4

Tandoori Shrimp

2 cloves garlic, minced

1 piece fresh ginger, about 2 inches (5 cm) long, peeled and cut up

3 tablespoons lemon or lime juice, plus lemon or lime wedges for garnish

1 tablespoon ground cumin

½ teaspoon salt

¼ teaspoon ground turmeric

2 jalapeño chiles, seeded, if desired, and minced

1 cup (8 oz/250 g) plain nonfat yogurt

1 tablespoon paprika, plus paprika for garnish

1½ lb (750 g) large shrimp (prawns), peeled and deveined

The shrimp can also be skewered and cooked in a preheated broiler (griller), or they can be sautéed in unsalted butter or peanut or olive oil. Soak the skewers while the charcoal heats in the grill.

❧

In a food processor or a blender, combine the garlic, ginger, lemon or lime juice, cumin, salt, turmeric, jalapeños, yogurt, and 1 tablespoon paprika. Process until well blended. Transfer to a nonaluminum bowl, add the shrimp, and toss to coat evenly. Cover and refrigerate for about 1 hour.

Prepare a fire in a charcoal grill. Place 12 bamboo skewers in water to cover and soak for 15–30 minutes.

Drain the skewers, then remove the shrimp from the marinade. Holding 2 skewers parallel and holding the shrimp flat, thread 4 or 5 of the shrimp onto the pair of skewers. (Parallel skewers make turning the shrimp on the grill easier.) Repeat with the remaining shrimp and skewers.

Place on an oiled grill rack and grill for 2 minutes. Turn the shrimp and grill until they turn pink, about 2 minutes longer.

Sprinkle with paprika and serve immediately with lemon or lime wedges.

Serves 6

Roast Leg of Lamb with Braised Garlic, Sherry, and Thyme

1 leg of lamb, about 6 lb (3 kg)
3 or 4 cloves garlic, slivered
12–14 small fresh thyme sprigs, each
  ½ inch (12 mm) long
salt and ground pepper to taste

FOR THE BRAISED GARLIC:
3 heads garlic, cloves separated and
  peeled
beef broth, to cover
3 fresh thyme sprigs
1 bay leaf

FOR THE SAUCE:
beef broth as needed
1 cup (8 fl oz/250 ml) dry sherry
4 teaspoons chopped fresh thyme
salt and ground pepper to taste

Cut 12–14 small, shallow slits into the surface of the lamb. Insert a garlic sliver and a thyme sprig into each slit. Cover and refrigerate for up to 1 day. Remove the lamb from the refrigerator about an hour before putting it in the oven.

Preheat an oven to 400°F (200°C). Sprinkle the lamb with salt and pepper and place in a roasting pan. Roast until an instant-read thermometer inserted into the thickest part away from the bone registers registers 130°–135°F (54°–57°C) or the meat is pink when cut with sharp knife, about 1¼ hours.

While the lamb is roasting, prepare the braised garlic: In a saucepan over medium heat, combine the garlic cloves, broth to cover barely, thyme sprigs, and bay leaf. Cover, bring to a simmer, and continue to simmer over medium heat until the garlic is tender when pierced, about 25 minutes. Remove from the heat and, using a slotted spoon, transfer the garlic to a small bowl. Strain the cooking liquid into a 2-cup (16–fl oz/500-ml) measuring pitcher.

To make the sauce, add enough broth to the strained liquid to measure 2 cups (16 fl oz/500 ml) and transfer to a saucepan. Add the sherry and bring to a boil over high heat. Boil, uncovered, until reduced by one-third. Add the chopped thyme and reserved braised garlic cloves. Adjust the seasonings with salt and pepper and keep warm.

When the lamb is done, remove from the oven and cover loosely with aluminum foil. Let rest for 10 minutes. Carve the lamb and divide evenly among individual plates. Spoon some of the sauce, including the garlic cloves, over each serving. Serve immediately.

Serves 6–8

Steamed Mussels

3½–4 lb (1.75–2 kg) mussels, well scrubbed and debearded
¼ cup (2 oz/60 g) unsalted butter
¼ cup (1¼ oz/37 g) minced shallots
1 small bay leaf
1 tablespoon chopped fresh thyme
1 cup (8 fl oz/250 ml) dry white wine
6 tablespoons (½ oz/15 g) chopped fresh parsley
salt and ground pepper to taste
crusty French bread

This simple bowlful of shellfish is a classic of Parisian bistros, where crusty bread is always served to soak up the aromatic broth.

❧

Discard any mussels that do not close to the touch. In a large pot over medium-low heat, melt the butter. Add the shallots and sauté until translucent, 2–3 minutes. Add the bay leaf, thyme, and wine, raise the heat to medium-high, and cook for about 2 minutes. Add the mussels, scatter 4 tablespoons (⅓ oz/10 g) of the parsley over the top, and sprinkle with salt and pepper. Cover and cook, shaking the pot once or twice, until the mussels open, about 5 minutes.

Using a slotted spoon, transfer the mussels to 4 warmed soup plates or bowls, dividing them equally. Discard any mussels that have not opened. Spoon the broth over the mussels and sprinkle with the remaining 2 tablespoons parsley. Serve immediately with French bread to sop up the juices. Provide small bowls at the table for discarding the shells.

Serves 4

Greek Beef Stew

½ cup (4 fl oz/120 ml) olive oil

3 lb (1.5 kg) beef chuck, cut into 2-inch
   (5-cm) cubes

salt and ground pepper to taste

2 large yellow onions, chopped

6 cloves garlic, minced

2 teaspoons ground cinnamon

1 teaspoon ground cloves

3 cups (24 fl oz/750 ml) dry red wine

10 plum (Roma) tomatoes, peeled,
   seeded, and chopped (fresh or canned),
   or 3 cups (24 fl oz/750 ml) canned
   tomato purée

2 bay leaves

2 lb (1 kg) pearl onions, unpeeled

¾ cup (4 oz/125 g) dried currants

Sweet and aromatic with currants, cinnamon, cloves, and tomatoes, this Greek beef stew is best served with oven-roasted potatoes or pilaf. Crumbled feta cheese makes a flavorful garnish. The stew can simmer on the stove top or in the oven. If you have time, marinate the beef, which will give it more flavor.

❧

*I*n a frying pan over high heat, warm ¼ cup (2 fl oz/60 ml) of the oil. Sprinkle the meat with salt and pepper and brown on all sides, 10–15 minutes. Remove from the heat and set aside.

In a large, heavy pot over medium heat, warm the remaining ¼ cup (2 fl oz/60 ml) oil. Add the chopped onions and sauté until tender and translucent, 10–15 minutes. Add the garlic, cinnamon, and cloves and cook for a few more minutes. Add the browned beef cubes, wine, tomatoes or tomato purée, and bay leaves and bring to a boil. Reduce the heat to low, cover, and simmer until the meat is tender, 1½–2 hours.

Meanwhile, bring a saucepan three-fourths full of water to a boil. Add the pearl onions and boil for 2 minutes, then drain well. When cool, use a small, sharp knife to trim off their root ends. Slip off the skins by squeezing gently with your fingers.

Add the onions and currants to the stew during the last 45 minutes of cooking. Taste the stew and adjust the seasonings just before serving.

Serves 6

Ginger-and-Orange-Curried Fried Chicken

2 cups (16 fl oz/500 ml) buttermilk
3 tablespoons grated orange zest
2 tablespoons peeled and grated fresh
  ginger
salt and ground black pepper to taste
12 boneless chicken breast halves, 5–6 oz
  (155–185 g) each
1½ cups (7½ oz/235 g) all-purpose
  (plain) flour
4–5 teaspoons curry powder
¾ teaspoon ground ginger
pinch of cayenne pepper (optional)
peanut oil for deep-frying
mango chutney

Although frying the chicken must be done at the last minute, it marinates in the refrigerator for about 2 hours. Buttermilk and ginger tenderize the meat, so do not allow the chicken to stand in the marinade longer than the specified time. Look for mango chutney in well-stocked food stores.

❦

*I*n a shallow nonaluminum dish or pan, combine the buttermilk, grated orange zest, ginger, and salt and black pepper and mix well. Add the chicken, turning to coat well. Cover and refrigerate for 1–2 hours.

In a large paper bag or on a deep plate, combine the flour, curry powder, ground ginger, salt, black pepper, and cayenne pepper, if using.

Remove the chicken pieces from the marinade and, a few pieces at a time, shake them in the bag of seasoned flour or coat them evenly in the seasoned flour on the plate.

In a large frying pan (or in 2 pans) over medium heat, pour in oil to a depth of 3 inches (7.5 cm). Heat to 375°F (190°C), or until a small cube of bread turns golden within moments of being dropped into it. When the oil is ready, add the chicken pieces and fry, turning once, until golden brown on the exterior and opaque at the center, 3–4 minutes on each side.

Using a slotted spatula, transfer to paper towels to drain briefly. Arrange on a warmed platter or individual plates and serve immediately with the chutney.

Serves 6

Bing Cherry Cheese Tart

2 cups (8 oz/250 g) stemmed Bing
   cherries, pitted
2 tablespoons Tuaca or amaretto or
   Frangelico

FOR THE TART SHELL PASTRY:
1¼ cups (6½ oz/200 g) all-purpose
   (plain) flour
¼ cup (2 oz/60 g) sugar
½ cup (4 oz/125 g) chilled unsalted
   butter, slivered
1 egg yolk
2 tablespoons heavy (double) cream
1 tablespoon Tuaca or amaretto or
   Frangelico
1 teaspoon grated lemon zest

FOR THE CHEESE FILLING:
½ lb (250 g) cream cheese, at room
   temperature
⅓ cup (3 oz/90 g) sugar
2 whole eggs or 1 whole egg and
   2 egg yolks
2 tablespoons Tuaca or amaretto or
   Frangelico
½ teaspoon almond extract (essence)

In a bowl, toss together the cherries and liqueur. Cover and let stand for 4 hours to blend the flavors.

To make the tart shell pastry, in a bowl, stir together the flour and sugar. Using 2 knives or a pastry blender, cut in the butter until the mixture resembles cornmeal. In a small bowl, whisk together the egg yolk, cream, liqueur, and lemon zest. Add to the flour mixture and, using a fork, stir together until the dough forms a rough mass. Gather the dough into a ball, flatten it, and wrap in plastic wrap. Chill for at least 1 hour or for up to 1 day.

Preheat an oven to 400°F (200°C).

On a well-floured surface, roll out the pastry into a round about 11 inches (28 cm) in diameter. Carefully transfer the round to a 9-inch (23-cm) tart pan with a removable bottom. If the dough is difficult to roll out, press by hand into the tart pan. Do not fit the dough too snugly to the pan, as the crust will shrink as it bakes. Make the sides slightly higher than the pan rim, then trim off any excess overhang. Using a fork, prick a few holes in the bottom of the crust. Line with aluminum foil and fill with pie weights. Bake for 15 minutes, then remove the weights and foil. Reduce the oven temperature to 350°F (180°C) and bake until lightly colored, about 15 minutes longer. Transfer to a wire rack to cool. Leave the oven set at 350°F (180°C).

Meanwhile, to make the cheese filling, in a bowl, combine the cream cheese, sugar, whole eggs or whole egg and egg yolks, liqueur, and almond extract. Using an electric mixer, beat until well combined.

Distribute the cherries evenly on the bottom of the tart shell. Pour the cheese mixture over the cherries. Bake until the custard is set, about 25 minutes. Let cool on a wire rack, then cut into wedges and serve.

Serves 6–8

Mexican Wedding Cookies

1 cup (4 oz/125 g) pecans

1 cup (8 oz/250 g) unsalted butter, at
 room temperature

⅓ cup (3 oz/90 g) granulated sugar

1 teaspoon vanilla extract (essence)

grated zest of 2 oranges

¼ cup (2 fl oz/60 ml) orange juice

2 egg yolks

3 cups (15 oz/470 g) all-purpose (plain)
 flour

1 cup (4 oz/125 g) confectioners' (icing)
 sugar

These cookies can be baked and coated with confectioners' sugar 2 days before serving and stored in an airtight container at room temperature. Uncoated cookies can be kept in an airtight tin for up to 1 week. Dust with sugar just before serving.

Preheat an oven to 350°F (180°C). Spread the pecans on a baking sheet and toast until lightly colored and fragrant, 5–7 minutes. Remove from the oven, let cool, and, using a nut grinder or food processor, grind finely. Set aside.

In a large bowl, combine the butter and granulated sugar. Using an electric mixer, beat the mixture, scraping down the sides of the bowl occasionally, until it is fluffy and light, 5–8 minutes. Add the vanilla, orange zest and juice, and egg yolks and continue to beat until fully incorporated.

Reduce the speed to low and beat in the flour, one-third at a time, beating well after each addition. Stir in the ground pecans. The dough should be soft and light. Cover the bowl and refrigerate the dough until slightly chilled, about 30 minutes.

Preheat an oven to 350°F (180°C). Line a baking sheet with parchment (baking) paper. Using a teaspoon, scoop up the dough and roll it between your palms into 1-inch (2.5-cm) balls. Arrange the balls, well spaced, on the prepared baking sheet.

Bake until golden, about 10 minutes. Remove from the oven and transfer to wire racks to cool for a few minutes. Roll as many warm cookies as you think will be eaten within 2 days in confectioners' sugar to coat evenly. Let coated and uncoated cookies cool completely on wire racks before storing.

Makes about 3 dozen

Dried Apricot Compote

1½ lb (750 g) dried apricots

⅓ cup (2 oz/60 g) golden raisins (sultanas)

5–6 cups (40–48 fl oz/1.25–1.5 l) water or Riesling, Moscato, or other sweet wine

1 cup (8 oz/250 g) sugar, or to taste

2 orange zest strips

½ teaspoon ground cardamom

¾ cup (4 oz/125 g) pine nuts or slivered almonds (optional)

1–2 tablespoons orange flower water or rose water

Dried fruits make a wonderful dessert compote in winter. If you like, a mixture of dried fruits can be used in place of the apricots and raisins. Prepare the compote up to 3 days ahead of serving.

In a bowl, combine the apricots, raisins, and enough water or wine to cover. Let stand overnight at room temperature. The next morning, transfer the fruits and their soaking liquid to a saucepan and add additional water or wine as needed to cover. Add the sugar, orange zest, and cardamom and bring to a boil, stirring to dissolve the sugar. Reduce the heat to medium and simmer, uncovered, until the apricots are tender, about 30 minutes.

Meanwhile, if using the nuts, preheat an oven to 350°F (180°C). Spread the nuts on a baking sheet and toast until lightly colored and fragrant, 5–7 minutes. Remove from the oven and let cool.

Remove the fruit from the heat and stir in orange flower water or rose water to taste and the nuts, if using. Transfer to a bowl, let cool, cover, and chill before serving.

Serves 4

Bittersweet Chocolate Cake

3 tablespoons cake (soft-wheat) flour

1 tablespoon cocoa

2 teaspoons instant espresso powder

5 oz (155 g) bittersweet chocolate,
  chopped into chunks

6 tablespoons (3 oz/90 g) unsalted butter,
  cut into small cubes, at room
  temperature

4 eggs, separated

½ cup (3½ oz/105 g) superfine (caster)
  sugar

1 teaspoon vanilla extract (essence)

FOR THE WHIPPED CREAM TOPPING:

1 cup (8 fl oz/250 ml) heavy (double)
  cream

2 tablespoons sour cream

2 tablespoons confectioners' (icing) sugar

1 tablespoon finely grated orange zest

1 teaspoon vanilla extract (essence)

confectioners' (icing) sugar for dusting

*True chocolate purists will love this cake. It has a fine flavor without
being too rich, and it does not need an icing. The cake tastes best when
served warm. Reheat leftovers in a 220° F (93° C) oven for 4–5 minutes.*

Preheat an oven to 350°F (180°C). Butter and flour an 8-inch
(20-cm) springform pan with 2-inch (5-cm) sides.

In a bowl, sift together the flour, cocoa, and espresso powder.
Set aside.

Place the chocolate in a heatproof bowl and set over (but not
touching) barely simmering water in a saucepan. Melt, stirring
occasionally, then remove from the heat and stir in the butter, a
little at a time, until blended. Let cool slightly.

In a large bowl, combine the egg yolks and superfine sugar.
Using an electric mixer set on medium speed, beat until creamy,
3–4 minutes. Beat in the chocolate mixture until blended. Fold in
the flour mixture and then the vanilla.

Beat the egg whites until soft peaks form. Stir one-fourth of the
whites into the batter. Fold in the remaining whites just until no
white streaks remain. Pour into the prepared pan and level the top.

Bake until the top is risen and crusty and a toothpick inserted
into the center comes out almost clean, 30–35 minutes. The
center should be soft and moist. Let cool on a wire rack for 10–15
minutes. The top will fall a bit. Remove the pan sides. Loosen the
edges of the cake with a knife and slide the warm cake onto a
serving plate.

To make the topping, in a bowl, whisk together the cream and
sour cream until slightly thickened. Beat in the sugar, orange zest,
and vanilla until soft folds form.

Dust the warm cake with confectioners' sugar. Cut into slices
and top with the whipped cream.

Serves 6–8

Caramelized Pumpkin Flan

¾ cup (6 oz/185 g) sugar

1½ tablespoons water

¾ cup (6 fl oz/180 ml) light (single) cream

½ cup (4 oz/125 g) pumpkin purée

grated zest of 1 small orange

½ teaspoon ground cinnamon

¼ teaspoon ground ginger

pinch of ground nutmeg

pinch of salt

2 eggs, lightly beaten

½ teaspoon vanilla extract (essence)

A good way to use leftover pumpkin, this classic dessert is easy to prepare and best when made the day before serving. Mashed cooked sweet potatoes can be used in place of the pumpkin.

Preheat an oven to 325°F (165°C).

In a small saucepan over low heat, combine ½ cup (4 oz/125 g) of the sugar and the water, stirring until the sugar dissolves. Raise the heat to high and cook without stirring until the liquid is caramel colored and has a faintly burnt aroma, 6–8 minutes; do not allow it to burn. Remove from the heat and pour carefully into the bottom of four ½-cup (4–fl oz/125-ml) custard cups or ceramic ramekins, tilting them to coat the bottoms and sides. Set aside.

In a saucepan over medium heat, warm the cream until tiny bubbles form along the edge of the pan; do not allow to boil. Meanwhile, in a bowl, combine the pumpkin, remaining ¼ cup (2 oz/60 g) sugar, orange zest, cinnamon, ginger, nutmeg, and salt. Stir to mix well, then stir in the eggs. Gradually stir in the hot cream, a little at a time, and then the vanilla. Stir until smooth and pour into the prepared dishes. Place in a baking pan and pour hot water into the pan to reach halfway up the sides of the dishes. Cover the pan with aluminum foil.

Bake until set and a knife inserted in the center of a flan comes out clean, about 45 minutes. Remove from the water bath and let rest on a wire rack for about 30 minutes, then cover and chill well.

At serving time, run a knife around the inside edge of each dish and invert each flan onto a plate or shallow bowl. Serve at once.

Serves 4

Hazelnut Biscotti

2 cups (10 oz/315 g) hazelnuts (filberts)

2½ cups (12½ oz/390 g) all-purpose (plain) flour

1½ teaspoons baking powder

1 teaspoon ground cinnamon

½ teaspoon salt

½ cup (4 oz/125 g) unsalted butter, at room temperature

1 cup (8 oz/250 g) sugar

3 eggs

juice and grated zest of 1 lemon

1 tablespoon vanilla extract (essence)

½ teaspoon almond extract (essence)

These cookies can be made 5 days before serving and stored in an airtight container. If they soften, recrisp them in a 250° F (120° C) oven.

Preheat an oven to 325°F (165°C). Spread the hazelnuts on a baking sheet and toast until lightly colored and fragrant, and the skins split and loosen, 5–10 minutes. Remove from the oven, let cool for a few minutes, then wrap in a clean kitchen towel. Rub against them with your palms to remove most of the skins. Do not worry if small bits remain. Chop the nuts coarsely and set aside. Leave the oven set at 325°F (165°C).

In a bowl, stir together the flour, baking powder, cinnamon, and salt. Set aside. In another bowl, combine the butter and sugar. Using an electric mixer set on medium speed, beat the mixture until light and fluffy. Add the eggs, one at a time, beating well after each addition. Beat in the lemon juice and zest and vanilla and almond extracts. Reduce the speed to low and beat in the flour mixture, one-third at a time. Fold in the nuts. The dough will be slightly granular.

Turn the dough out onto a floured work surface and divide it in half. Using your palms, roll each half into an oval log about 1½ inches (4 cm) in diameter. Place well spaced on an ungreased baking sheet.

Bake until golden brown, about 30 minutes. Remove from the oven and let rest until cool to the touch. Reduce the oven temperature to 250°F (120°C).

Cut each log on the diagonal into slices ⅓ inch (1 cm) thick. Arrange the slices, cut side down, on the ungreased baking sheet and return to the oven. Bake until lightly toasted and the edges are golden brown, about 10 minutes. Let cool either on the baking sheet or on a wire rack.

Makes 18–20

Chocolate Mousse

½ teaspoon instant espresso powder
1 tablespoon boiling water
⅛ teaspoon ground cardamom
4 oz (125 g) bittersweet chocolate,
    preferably a dark, rich chocolate,
    broken or chopped into small pieces
2 tablespoons unsalted butter
4 eggs, separated
1 tablespoon sugar
⅛ teaspoon cream of tartar
strips of candied orange peel

Take care not to overbeat the egg whites or they will become dry and start to break apart. Whites beaten with a light hand will mix most successfully into the chocolate, without losing much of their loft. The candied orange peel adds considerably to this dessert and is delicious eaten with after-dinner coffee. Look for candied peel in a specialty-food store.

In a cup, dissolve the espresso powder in the boiling water, stir in the ground cardamom, and set aside.

Place the chocolate and butter in a heatproof bowl and set over (but not touching) barely simmering water in a saucepan. Melt, stirring occasionally. When melted, add the espresso mixture and stir until blended and smooth. Remove from the heat.

In a separate bowl, combine the egg yolks and sugar. Whisk until increased in volume and very light, 3–4 minutes. While stirring the melted chocolate with a wooden spoon, gradually add the beaten yolks, then beat until the chocolate thickens.

Place the egg whites and cream of tartar in another clean, dry bowl. Using a clean whisk or beaters, beat until stiff peaks form that hold their shape but are not dry. Add about one-fourth of the beaten whites to the chocolate mixture and, using a rubber spatula, stir gently to blend. Then add the remaining egg whites and gently fold in just until no white streaks remain. Pour into a serving bowl. Cover the bowl with paper towels (this absorbs any condensation that forms); make sure the towels do not touch the mousse. Refrigerate for several hours until well set.

At the table, spoon the mousse into shallow bowls or deep plates. Place strips of candied orange peel alongside each serving.

Serves 4

Pear Clafouti

1½–2 lb (750 g–1 kg) ripe but firm Bosc
  or Anjou pears, peeled, halved, cored,
  and cut into 1-inch (2.5-cm) pieces
⅓ cup (3 fl oz/80 ml) pear brandy or
  ½ cup (4 fl oz/125 ml) sweet
  white wine
3 tablespoons minced crystallized ginger
  (optional)
2 tablespoons unsalted butter
3 eggs
½ cup (2½ oz/75 g) all-purpose (plain)
  flour
½ cup (4 oz/125 g) granulated sugar
½ teaspoon ground cinnamon (optional)
1 cup (8 fl oz/250 ml) milk
½ cup (4 fl oz/125 ml) heavy (double)
  cream
grated zest of 1 lemon or ½ orange
1 teaspoon vanilla extract (essence)
pinch of salt
confectioners’ (icing) sugar

*A clafouti is a rustic fruit “pancake” from the Limousin region of
France. It is traditionally prepared with cherries, but pears are a
delicious alternative.*

Preheat an oven to 375°F (190°C).

In a small saucepan over medium heat, combine the pears,
brandy or wine, and crystallized ginger, if using. Cook gently,
stirring occasionally, until the pears are tender but not mushy,
about 10 minutes.

Meanwhile, thoroughly grease a 10-inch (25-cm) pie pan or
other shallow round baking dish with the butter. When the pears
are ready, distribute them and their juices evenly on the bottom of
the prepared pan or dish.

In a blender or in a bowl, blend or whisk together the eggs,
flour, granulated sugar, cinnamon (if using), milk, cream, zest,
vanilla, and salt until well mixed. To eliminate any lumps, scrape
down the sides of the blender container or bowl and blend the
batter again. Let the batter rest for about 5 minutes.

Pour the batter evenly over the pears. Bake until puffed and set,
35–40 minutes. Remove from the oven and sift a light dusting of
confectioners’ sugar over the top. Serve warm.

Serves 6

Baked Apples

6 large Rome Beauty apples

grated zest of 1 orange

6 tablespoons (2 oz/60 g) chopped raisins

¼ cup (2 oz/60 g) firmly packed brown sugar

¼ cup (2 oz/60 g) unsalted butter, at room temperature

1 teaspoon ground cinnamon

¼ cup (3 oz/90 g) honey

½ cup (4 fl oz/125 ml) orange juice or apple cider

Few other desserts fill the house with such a wonderful fragrance as they cook. Look for Rome Beauty apples at your market, as they are the best for baking. The apples will hold their shape but will also become custardy inside. If you like, serve them with a dollop of cream, crème fraîche, sweetened plain yogurt, or vanilla ice cream. They can be baked up to 8 hours before serving and served at room temperature. Or, if you prefer, warm them in a 350°F (180°C) oven for 15 minutes.

Preheat an oven to 350°F (180°C).

Core the apples to within ½ inch (12 mm) of the base. Then peel them only halfway down from the top. Place side by side in a baking dish.

In a small bowl, stir together the orange zest, raisins, brown sugar, butter, and cinnamon until well mixed. Divide this mixture evenly among the apples, pushing it down into the apple cavities.

In a small saucepan over medium-low heat, combine the honey and orange juice or cider. Heat just until the honey dissolves. Pour the honey mixture evenly over the apples. Bake the apples, basting often with the pan juices, until tender when pierced, about 45 minutes.

To serve, let cool to room temperature. Place on individual plates and spoon the pan juices over the top.

Serves 6

Peach Bread Pudding

6 tablespoons (3 oz/90 g) unsalted butter, melted and clarified

12 slices fine-textured white bread or brioche, cut into 1-inch (2.5-cm) cubes

4 cups (32 fl oz/1 l) heavy (double) cream

6 large, ripe peaches, peeled, pitted, and cut into ¾-inch (2-cm) cubes

¼ cup (2 fl oz/60 ml) amaretto liqueur

4 whole eggs, plus 4 egg yolks

¾ cup (6 oz/185 g) sugar

1 teaspoon vanilla extract (essence)

½ teaspoon almond extract (essence)

All you need for this delicate summer pudding is flavorful ripe peaches. The almond-scented amaretto liqueur gives the fruit a pleasing fragrance and flavor. The pudding can be baked up to 6 hours ahead.

In a large frying pan over medium-high heat, melt 3 tablespoons of the butter. Add half of the bread cubes and fry, stirring, until golden on all sides, 3–4 minutes. Using a slotted spoon, transfer to paper towels to drain. Repeat with 3 more tablespoons butter and the remaining bread cubes.

In a saucepan over medium heat, warm the cream until small bubbles appear along the edge of the pan. Meanwhile, in a bowl, combine the peaches and amaretto and toss to coat.

In another bowl, combine the whole eggs, egg yolks, and sugar and, using a whisk, beat until frothy. Whisk about ½ cup (4 fl oz/ 125 ml) of the hot cream into the egg mixture, then gradually whisk in the remaining cream. Stir in the vanilla and almond extracts. To remove any lumps, pour the mixture through a fine-mesh sieve into a clean pitcher or bowl.

Combine the peaches and bread cubes in a 3-qt (3-l) shallow rectangular or oval baking dish. Mix to distribute evenly. Slowly pour in the custard, being careful not to disturb the peach mixture. Place the baking dish in a large roasting pan and pour hot water into the pan to reach halfway up the sides of the dish.

Bake until the custard is just set, about 1½ hours; it should still be slightly wobbly in the center.

Let cool on a wire rack before serving.

Serves 6

Banbury Tart

FOR THE TART SHELL PASTRY:

1¼ cups (6½ oz/200 g) all-purpose (plain) flour

1 tablespoon sugar

¼ teaspoon salt

½ cup (4 oz/125 g) chilled unsalted butter, slivered

2 tablespoons cold water, or as needed

1½ cups (9 oz/280 g) raisins

1 cup (8 fl oz/250 ml) water

⅔ cup (5 oz/155 g) sugar

4 soda crackers, finely crushed

2 teaspoons grated lemon zest

2 tablespoons lemon juice

1 egg, beaten

FOR THE TOPPING:

½ cup (2½ oz/75 g) all-purpose (plain) flour

3 tablespoons unsalted butter

2 tablespoons sugar

¼ teaspoon salt

To make the tart shell pastry, in a bowl, stir together the flour, sugar, and salt. Using 2 knives or a pastry blender, cut in the butter until the mixture has the consistency of rolled oats. Sprinkle 1 tablespoon of the water over the flour mixture, then stir and toss with a fork. Sprinkle on another tablespoon water and stir until the mixture comes together in a rough mass. If it will not hold together, add a few more drops water. Gather the dough into a ball, flatten it, and wrap in plastic wrap. Refrigerate for at least 30 minutes.

Preheat an oven to 400°F (200°C).

On a well-floured surface, roll out the pastry to line a 9-inch (23-cm) round or square tart pan with a removable bottom. Carefully transfer to the pan and trim off any excess overhang. Using a fork, prick a few holes in the bottom and sides of the shell. Line the tart shell with aluminum foil and fill with pie weights. Bake for 8 minutes, then remove the weights and foil. Continue to bake until the pastry looks dry but is still very pale, about 4 minutes longer. Let cool completely before filling.

In a heavy-bottomed saucepan over high heat, combine the raisins, water, sugar, crackers and lemon zest. Bring to a boil, stirring to dissolve the sugar. Reduce the heat to low and simmer until slightly thickened, about 10 minutes. Remove from the heat and stir in the lemon juice and egg; set aside.

To make the topping, in a small bowl, combine the flour, butter, sugar, and salt. Using your fingertips, blend together until the mixture resembles fine crumbs.

Pour the raisin mixture into the cooled tart shell and sprinkle the crumb mixture evenly over the top. Bake until lightly browned on top, about 35 minutes. Let cool on a wire rack before serving.

Serves 6–8

Glossary

The following glossary defines terms both generally and as they relate specifically to casual entertaining, including major and unusual ingredients and basic techniques.

ANCHOVIES
These tiny saltwater fish, related to the sardine, add intense, briny flavor to dishes in which they are used. They are usually sold as canned fillets that have been salted and packed in oil. Imported fillets in olive oil are the best choice for the recipes in this book.

ARTICHOKES
The flower buds of a type of thistle native to the Mediterranean. Their cluster of tough, pointed leaves covers pale green inner leaves and a prickly, inedible choke that tops a tender, gray-green base. Baby artichokes need only light trimming of their outer leaves before they are cooked and eaten whole.

To trim baby artichokes, break off the tough outer leaves to reveal the pale green inner leaves. Using a sharp knife, cut off the stem even with the base, then cut off the top half of the artichoke. Rub the cut surfaces with a lemon half as you work and immerse the trimmed artichokes in a bowl of water containing lemon juice until ready to use.

ASPARAGUS
Member of the lily family that produces long, slender stalks with a compact bud at one end. The most common variety is green; white spears are occasionally available in well-stocked markets and greengrocers. Boiled until tender-crisp, asparagus are served cold in salads or hot as a side dish.

To trim asparagus, cut or snap off any tough, woody ends from the spears and discard. If the spears are thick, using a vegetable peeler and starting about 2 inches (5 cm) below the tip, peel off the skin.

BALSAMIC VINEGAR
A specialty of Modena, Italy, balsamic vinegar is made from reduced grape juice and is aged many years. Its sweet, pungent flavor is appreciated in vinaigrettes for salads and grilled vegetables.

BELL PEPPERS
Sweet-fleshed, bell-shaped members of the pepper family. They

are most commonly sold in the unripe green form; ripened red or yellow varieties are also available. Also known as capsicums.

To prepare a raw bell pepper, cut it in half lengthwise with a sharp knife. Pull out the stem section from each half, along with the cluster of seeds attached to it. Remove any remaining seeds and any thin white membranes, or ribs, to which they are attached. Cut the pepper halves as directed in specific recipes.

BREAD CRUMBS
Bread crumbs add body to meatballs and other preparations, form a coating for fried foods, and create a crunchy golden topping on baked dishes.

To make fresh crumbs, select a good-quality coarse country bread. Cut away the crusts and crumble the bread by hand or in a blender or a food processor. For dried crumbs, dry the fresh crumbs in an oven set at its lowest temperature for about 1 hour. Alternatively, purchase packaged crumbs in food stores.

BUTTER, CLARIFIED
Unsalted butter from which the milk solids have been removed, thereby enabling it to be used to cook foods at high temperatures without burning.

To make clarified butter, melt unsalted butter in a small frying pan over low heat. Skim off the froth from the surface. Pour off the clear yellow clarified butter, then discard the milky solids that remain in the pan.

CARDAMOM
Sweet, exotic-tasting spice used in both sweet and savory dishes. Its small, round seeds come enclosed in a husklike pod. Cardamom is best purchased whole, then ground with a spice grinder or with a mortar and pestle as needed.

CHUTNEY
Refers to numerous spiced East Indian relishes or pickles served as condiments with meals and used as seasonings in cooking. Most common are fruit-based chutneys such as mango, which are sold in ethnic markets and well-stocked food stores.

CLOVES
Rich and aromatic spice used whole or in its ground form.

CRÈME FRAÎCHE
This French-style lightly soured and thickened fresh cream is increasingly available in well-stocked markets. A similar product may be prepared at home by lightly whipping 1 cup (8 fl oz/ 250 ml) heavy (double) cream, then stirring in 2 teaspoons sour cream. Or, to make your own crème fraîche, stir 1 teaspoon cultured buttermilk into 1 cup (8 fl oz/250 ml) heavy cream. Cover tightly and leave at warm room temperature until thickened, about 12 hours. Refrigerate the crème fraîche for up to 1 week until ready to serve.

CUCUMBERS
Belonging to the squash family, cucumbers have a dark green skin that conceals a juicy, pale green flesh with a refreshing flavor and texture appreciated in salads and cold soups. The bitter skins of most cucumbers need to be peeled,

and the seeds removed from the flesh. The long, thin English cucumber, also called hothouse cucumber, has few if any seeds and the skin is usually edible.

HERBS

All manner of herbs, both fresh and dried, serve as seasonings and garnishes. Among the most common types, used in this book, are:

Basil Sweet, spicy herb popular in Italian and French cooking, particularly as a seasoning for tomatoes.

Bay leaves Dried whole leaves of the bay laurel tree. They add an appealing pungent and spicy flavor to stocks and other simmered dishes. The French variety has a milder, sweeter flavor than California bay leaves.

Chives Mild, sweet herb with a fine, grasslike appearance and the subtle flavor of onion, to which it is related.

Cilantro Green, leafy herb resembling flat-leaf (Italian) parsley, with a sharp, somewhat astringent flavor. Also known as fresh coriander or Chinese parsley.

Dill Herb with fine, feathery leaves and a sweet, aromatic flavor, used in vegetable dishes.

Mint Refreshing sweet herb used fresh to season or garnish salads, soups, vegetables, and grain dishes.

Parsley A popular herb available in two main varieties. Flat-leaf parsley, also known as Italian parsley, is preferred for its pronounced flavor. This and the curly-leaf type are commonly available fresh in most food stores.

Rosemary A member of the mint family with strong-flavored, needlelike leaves, particularly well suited for use with poultry.

Sage Herb with a pungent flavor that complements vegetables and poultry.

Thyme Fragrant, cleantasting, small-leaved herb. A variety called lemon thyme has a subtle lemon scent and taste.

CUMIN

Middle Eastern spice whose strong, dusky, aromatic flavor enhances vinaigrettes and spice rubs. Cumin is sold ground or as small, crescent-shaped seeds that can be ground with a spice grinder or in a mortar with a pestle as needed.

CURRY POWDER

Generic term for blends of spices commonly used to flavor Indian-style dishes. Most blends contain coriander, cumin, ground chile, fenugreek, and turmeric. Some may also include cardamom, cinnamon, cloves, allspice, fennel seeds, and ginger.

DIJON MUSTARD

One of numerous mustards produced in France, Dijon mustard is made in and around the city of Dijon from dark brown mustard seeds (or from light seeds and marked *blanc*) and white wine or wine vinegar. Both Dijon mustard and non-French blends labeled Dijon style are fairly hot and sharp tasting.

EGGPLANTS

These mildly earthy, sweet vegetable-fruits have creamy white flesh and a tough, shiny skin, which may be peeled or left intact in grilled or long-cooked dishes. The skin varies in color from purple to red to white. The purple globe eggplant (above) is the most common variety. Also known as aubergine.

ESCAROLE

Variety of chicory with broad, curly, bright green leaves with a refreshingly bitter flavor. Used raw in salads and cooked. Also known as Batavian endive.

ESPRESSO POWDER, INSTANT

Instant espresso powder or granules provide an easily blended source of intense coffee flavor to baked goods. Available in the coffee section of well-stocked food stores, Italian delicatessens, and specialty-coffee stores.

FILO

Tissue-thin sheets of flour-and-water pastry used throughout the Middle East as crisp wrappers for savory or sweet fillings. Usually found in the frozen food section of well-stocked food stores or can be purchased fresh in Middle Eastern delicatessens. To use frozen filo, defrost thoroughly in the refrigerator before use.

Whether fresh or thawed frozen, the fragile sheets, which generally measure about 10 by 14 inches (25 by 35 cm), must be separated and handled carefully to avoid tearing. As you work, keep the unused sheets covered with a lightly dampened kitchen towel to prevent drying.

GINGER

The knobby rhizome of the tropical ginger plant. Whole ginger rhizomes, commonly but mistakenly called roots, are usually purchased fresh. Peeled before use, they are used to add a pungent, spicy flavor to vinaigrettes, marinades, and basting sauces.

GREEN BEANS

Also known as string beans or snap beans, these fresh beans are picked when their pods and the seeds inside are immature, still tender, and edible. The Blue Lake variety is particularly favored for its bright color and crisp texture.

JALAPEÑO CHILE

Extremely hot fresh chile with a distinctively sharp flavor. Broad and tapered, the jalapeño measures about 1½ inches (4 cm) long and is usually dark green, although ripe red ones are occasionally available.

JUNIPER BERRIES

Aromatic, small dried berries of the juniper tree. They are used as a seasoning in spice rubs and marinades.

MAPLE SYRUP

Syrup made from boiling the sap of the maple tree, with an inimitably rich flavor and intense sweetness. Buy syrup that is labeled "pure," rather than a blend.

MUSHROOMS

With the meaty textures and rich flavors, mushrooms make substantial first courses and are used in classic pasta sauces. Cultivated white mushrooms, the most commonly available variety, have white caps and white stems. The smallest white mushrooms, with their caps still closed, are often called button mushrooms (below). Subtly flavored chanterelles are pale yellow, trumpet-shaped mushrooms 2–3 inches (5–7.5 cm) in length. Shiitakes are meaty-flavored Asian mushrooms with flat, dark brown caps. Richly flavored porcini, also known by the French term *cèpes*, are available fresh and, most commonly, dried. Cremini are cultivated mushrooms with brown caps. Portobellos, the mature form of the cremini, have large, dark brown caps, 4–6 inches (10–15 cm) in diameter; they are appreciated for their particularly robust texture.

NUTS

An array of nuts are used to add their crisp, crunchy texture to both sweet and savory dishes.

Almonds Mellow, sweet, oval-shaped nuts, sold whole (with their skins intact) and blanched (with their skins removed) and thinly sliced (flaked).

Hazelnuts Small, usually spherical nuts with a slightly sweet flavor. Also known as filberts.

Pecans Brown-skinned nuts with a distinctive, sweet, rich flavor, crisp, slightly crumbly texture, and crinkly surface.

PINE NUTS

Small, ivory seeds from the cones of a species of pine tree and possessing a rich, subtly resinous flavor.

Walnuts Rich, crisp nuts with distinctively crinkled surfaces. English walnuts are the most familiar variety; the largest crops are in California.

OLIVE OILS

The most flavorful olive oil is extra virgin, extracted from olives on the first pressing without use of heat or chemicals, and prized for its pure, fruity taste and golden to pale green hue. It is the preferred olive oil for vinaigrettes. Products labeled "pure olive oil" are milder in aroma and flavor and may be used for all-purpose cooking.

OLIVES

These small fruits of trees native to the Mediterranean and cultivated in other regions are cured and sold by the pound or in bottles or cans. For the recipes in this book, seek out Mediterranean-style black or green olives cured in brine, vinegar, oil, and other seasonings. Among the varieties available in well-stocked food stores and delicatessens are the small, salt-cured Gaeta; the brine-cured, vinegar-packed Kalamata; the brine-cured Sicilian, and the sun-dried, oil-cured Moroccan.

ORANGE FLOWER WATER

Intense flavoring made from orange blossoms and used in desserts. Available in well-stocked food stores and Middle Eastern delicatessens.

PANCETTA

An unsmoked bacon that has been cured simply with salt and pepper. It is available in Italian delicatessens and well-stocked food stores.

PEARS

Several pear varieties are available seasonally in well-stocked food stores and greengrocers for use raw and in cooked dishes. Anjou pears, in season from

autumn through midspring, are rich in flavor, with a hint of spice and a smooth texture. Among the largest and plumpest of pears, they have short necks and thin, yellow-green skins. Bartlett pears, also called Williams' pears (above, right), are shaped like bells, with creamy yellow skins sometimes tinged in red and flesh that is juicy and mild tasting. All-red Bartlett pears are also available. Long, slender, tapered Bosc pears have yellow-and-russet skin and slightly grainy, solid-textured white flesh with a hint of acidity. A good cooking pear, the Bosc is sold from October through the winter. Sweet and juicy Comice pears (above, left) are round, short-necked fruits with greenish yellow skins tinged with red. They are available from autumn through early winter.

PITA BREAD

Flat, oval, yeast-leavened bread of Mediterranean origin, noteworthy for the pocket that it forms during baking. Pita bread is ideal for cutting into wedges and serving with dips or spreads as an appetizer.

PROSCIUTTO

A raw ham that is cured by dry-salting for 1 month, then air-drying in cool curing sheds for 6 months or longer. A specialty of Parma, Italy, it is often cut into tissue-thin slices that emphasize its deep pink color and intense flavor. Look for prosciutto in Italian delicatessens and well-stocked food stores.

RED PEPPER FLAKES

Spice consisting of coarsely ground flakes of dried red chiles, including the seeds, which add moderately hot flavor to sauces, vinaigrettes, and other dishes.

RICE

Member of the grass family grown around the world and used in both sweet and savory dishes. Long-grain white rice, the most popular type, consists of slender grains that steam to a light, fluffy consistency. Short-grain varieties have a creamier, stickier consistency when cooked. A versatile grain, rice is used in salads, side dishes such as pilaf, and desserts.

SAFFRON

Intensely aromatic, golden orange spice made from the dried stigmas of a species of crocus and used to perfume and color many classic Mediterranean dishes such as paella. Sold either as threads—the dried stigmas—or in powdered form. For the best quality, look for products labeled "pure saffron."

SALT

Various forms of salt are used as a seasoning. Kosher salt, a coarse-grained salt that does not contain additives, is less salty than table salt and is sometimes preferred for its flavor and texture. Sea salt, sold in coarse and fine grinds, is extracted from sea water and has a stronger flavor than table salt.

SHALLOTS

Small member of the onion family with brownish skin and white flesh tinged with purple. The flavor resembles a cross between sweet onion and garlic.

SHRIMP

Raw shrimp (prawns) are generally sold with the heads already removed but the shells still intact. Before cooking, they are usually peeled and their veinlike intestinal tracts removed.

To peel and devein shrimp, using your thumbs, split open the shrimp's thin shell along the concave side, between its two rows of legs. Peel away the shell, taking care to leave the last seg-

TOMATOES

When tomatoes are in season, use the best sun-ripened tomatoes you can find, from succulent beef-steak tomatoes to the heirloom varieties sold at farmers' markets. At other times of the year plum tomatoes, sometimes called Roma or egg tomatoes, are likely to have the best flavor and texture. For cooking, canned whole, diced, or chopped plum tomatoes are also good.

To peel fresh tomatoes, bring a saucepan of water to a boil. Using a small, sharp knife, cut out the core from the stem end of the tomato, then cut a shallow X in the skin at the tomato's base.

Submerge for about 20 seconds in the boiling water, then remove and cool in a bowl of cold water. Starting at the X, peel the skin from the tomato, using your fingertips and, if necessary, the knife blade.

ment with the tail fin intact and attached to the meat if specified in the recipe.

TURMERIC

Pungent, earthy-flavored ground spice that, like saffron, adds a vibrant yellow color to marinades and other dishes in which it is used.

ZEST

Thin, brightly colored, outermost layer of a citrus fruit's peel, containing most of its essential oils. It is a lively source of flavor when added to both sweet and savory dishes.

To remove zest, use a simple tool known as a zester, drawing its sharp-edged holes across the fruit's skin to remove the zest in thin strips. The fine holes on a handheld grater can also be used.

To remove zest in strips, hold the edge of a paring knife or vegetable peeler almost parallel to the fruit's skin and carefully cut off the zest. Take care not to remove any bitter white pith with it.

Index

ACKNOWLEDGMENTS

The following authors provided the recipes for this book: Joyce Goldstein: pages 17, 19, 20, 22, 26, 33, 34, 37, 38, 41, 44, 49, 50, 53, 57, 58, 63, 64, 67, 68, 73, 74, 79, 80, 83, 85, 86, 90, 93, 96, 98, 101; Chuck Williams: 13, 42, 47, 61, 70, 77, 89, 95; Scotto Sisters: pages 15, 25, 29, 30; John Phillip Carroll: page 102; and Norman Kolpas: page 55.

The publishers thank the following people for their generous assistance and support in producing this book: Desne Border, Ken DellaPenta, Julia Schlosser, Karen Nicks, Danielle Di Salvo, Elizabeth Ruegg, Nette Scott, William Shaw, and Elizabeth C. Davis. The following kindly lent props for the photography: Williams-Sonoma, Pottery Barn, Chuck Williams, Sue Fisher King, Biordi Art Imports, and Fillamento. The publishers also thank all the other individuals and organizations that provided props, locations, and other assistance in producing this book.